Thoughts on a I

S. J. Jerram

Alpha Editions

This edition published in 2023

ISBN : 9789357948845

Design and Setting By
Alpha Editions
www.alphaedis.com
Email - info@alphaedis.com

Contents

THOUGHTS ON A REVELATION.

Few persons can have observed attentively the various phases of public opinion on religious subjects during the last twenty years or more, without noticing a growing tendency to the accumulation of difficulties on the subject of Revelation. Geology, ethnology, mythical interpretation, critical investigation, and inquiries of other kinds, have raised their several difficulties; and, in consequence, infidels have rejoiced, candid inquirers have been perplexed, and even those who have held with firmness decided views on the distinctive character of the inspiration of the Bible, have sometimes found it difficult to satisfy their minds entirely, and to see clearly the grounds of their conclusions.

The writer of these pages does not propose to attempt a detailed reply to the various difficulties which have been raised. Answers to objections arising from the pursuit of particular sciences are most effectually given by those, who have made those sciences their study; nor can there be any doubt that, if the book of nature and the Bible spring from the same source, an increasing acquaintance with both will tend to show their harmony with each other, and to dispel the perplexities which p. 2have arisen from an imperfect acquaintance with either of them. It may be observed, too, that, as it requires special knowledge on the part of a writer to cope with special difficulties; so also does it demand acquirements, but rarely found, on the part of the reader, to appreciate the real value, both of the objections and answers which may be made on geological, critical, or other special grounds.

The writer thinks that there is another method of reply—a method which consists in giving as clear a view as can be had of the real character of the subject against which the objections are made; and this is the kind of answer which he proposes to attempt. The man who has a distinct and well defined knowledge of chemical, mathematical, or any other science, will not be greatly perplexed with difficulties which may be brought from other sciences, touching upon that with which he is acquainted. The knowledge which he possesses of his own particular science will enable him, in some instances, to perceive at once the weakness of the objections which are alleged; and, even when this is not the case, he will see such an harmonious proportion subsisting between the various parts of that branch of knowledge which he has been pursuing, and be so strongly convinced of the certainty of it, that he will be justly disposed to attribute to his own ignorance his inability to give satisfactory replies to those difficulties which he cannot dispose of. *Real* knowledge cannot of course be overthrown; and, although it is often difficult to decide what knowledge is of this description, the task of arriving at a tolerably correct conclusion with regard to such subjects as fall within the range of our faculties, must not be regarded as an hopeless one.

When clear definitions have been given, disputants p. 3have often found that there is no further room for discussion; and, even when this is not the case, the force of objections can, under such circumstances, be more accurately weighed, and the real points of attack and defence more clearly perceived. If a man were to say, in a mixed company, that there was no taste in an apple, many sensible men, unacquainted with his exact meaning, might be inclined to dispute the assertion, and to say that the statement was contrary to common experience; but, if he explained his meaning to be, that taste is a quality of a sentient being, and that there is nothing in the apple of this kind, or corresponding to it, everybody then would see the truth of his assertion, and all ground of dispute would be removed. We will take another case. Those who hold strong Protestant views frequently say, that the "religion of the Bible is the religion of Protestants." This, for most purposes, expresses their meaning forcibly and well, and the mind, in practice, usually supplies the necessary limitations. It does not, however, always happen that these limitations are consciously present to the mind, or that the person who practically receives the right impression might not be greatly puzzled by the subtle reasonings of objectors. The *dictum*, quoted above, does not mean, as might at first sight appear, that we are to make use of no other means than the Bible in the investigation of Divine truth, and that the wisdom of the present and past ages is to go for nothing. No one *could* thus isolate himself from other influences; and, if he could, it would not be *desirable*. What is really meant is, that all truth necessary for salvation is contained in the Bible, "so that whatsoever is not read therein, nor may be proved thereby, is not to be required of any man that it should be believed p. 4as an article of faith," etc.; in other words, that the Bible is the ultimate and sole standard of appeal. This of course may be, and is disputed; but, when the statement is put in a clear and well defined shape, many apparent objections vanish at once, and the real points of attack and defence are made evident. If, then, we can obtain ideas, on the subject of revelation, which shall be, upon the whole, distinct, and worthy of being received as true, much will be done to remove objections, and to satisfy a reasonable mind.

The proposed investigation will necessarily be, in some degree, of an *a priori* character; not, however, as we trust, so much so as to render it vague and without practical value. It will be *a priori*, inasmuch as it will not assume the existence of a revelation, and then proceed to examine its character. This would be to beg the question at issue. It will not be *a priori*, so far as it consists in instituting an inquiry into the faculties of the human mind, and their capacity to receive a revelation; and into this it will be found that the investigation will mainly resolve itself.

1. We may commence our inquiry into the subject by noticing, *that a knowledge of God, to be obtained in some way or other, seems almost essential to the well-being of man.* If it be granted, that there is such a Being—and few, it is presumed, would go so far as to deny this—it must be of great importance for us to know the relationship in which that Being stands to us, and we to Him. We can hardly suppose it possible that an Infinite Being, in some sense, as we suppose will be generally allowed, the Governor of the world, should not have an important relation to *all* other existences; much less, that the relation p. 5which He bears to *man*, the most noble existence of which we have any actual experience, should be of an insignificant character. Looking, too, upon man as a free and moral agent, accountable, as conscience declares, for his actions to his fellow-men, it seems almost certain that he must be also responsible for his acts in relation to the Deity. The general belief of mankind, in all ages and in all places, tends to the same conclusion; and, if it be admitted that there is an eternal world into which the consequences of our actions follow us, a knowledge of the relationship in which we stand to God becomes of still greater importance. But if this knowledge probably may be, and, should the general belief of the world have a foundation in fact, certainly is, of great importance, it can hardly be supposed that a God of love would allow us to remain in ignorance of it; and the question arises, *how it is to be obtained.*

It may be observed, first of all, that *the Deity does not, like other objects, come within the direct cognizance of our perceptive faculties.* We have an organization, by means of which we are enabled to perceive various objects around us; and, by travelling to other lands, we can obtain a knowledge of many things of which we had before been ignorant. We perceive also what is going on within us. The telescope and the microscope reveal to us wonders which, without their intervention, we could never have discovered. But we cannot through the instrumentality of any of our faculties perceive God. Travel where we will we cannot find Him out. No appliance of art has availed to disclose Him to us. If any philosophers conceive that they can intuitively gaze upon God, other philosophers declare their ignorance of any intuition of this kind, and assuredly the common people, p. 6who most stand in need of clear notions on the subject, and who would hardly be neglected by a beneficent God, are altogether unconscious of it. The knowledge of Him, therefore, if obtained at all, must be had in some other way.

But may not an adequate knowledge of God be obtained *by the exercise of the faculties of the human mind upon external nature, or in some other way?* The Apostle St. Paul says something which rather favours this view, when he declares that "the invisible things of Him from the creation of the world are clearly seen, being understood by the things that are made, even His eternal power and

Godhead; so that they are without excuse" (Rom. i. 20): and we believe that a considerable insight into the nature of God, and the probable character of His dealings with us may be obtained in the manner to which we have referred. Still we have only to look at the ever varying and degrading notions which have, at all times, prevailed in many parts of the world respecting the Divine Being, to perceive that a more clear method of obtaining knowledge about Him would, to say the least of it, be a most valuable boon. The method under consideration has not practically issued as we might have hoped that it would; and therefore there is reason to expect, that God might make use of some more direct way of communicating to us a knowledge of Himself.

Another possible mode of communicating a knowledge of God would be, *by implanting in the mind of man, an idea corresponding, so far as might be needful, to the nature of God.* But a belief in the existence of anything of this kind is open to several objections. If such an idea existed, it must, to answer the required end, be sufficiently clear and well defined to give at least a tolerably accurate p. 7notion of the Deity, and must also bring with it a well-grounded conviction of its correspondence to the reality. But the variety of opinions which have been entertained on the subject forbid us to believe that any such idea as this exists. Search as far as we can into our own minds, we are unable to discover anything approaching to such a notion of the Divinity. It appears too, that, notwithstanding some speculations as to time and space, which, in the opinion of some, bear a slightly exceptional character, there is no good reason to believe that we acquire other kinds of knowledge in the manner under consideration; and, if this be so, there is a strong presumption against a knowledge of the Deity being obtained in this way.

As however some confusion of mind not uncommonly prevails on this subject, we will endeavour to explain our meaning more fully. We possess, as it appears to us, certain capacities for obtaining knowledge, and for retaining, and disposing our knowledge, when obtained, in different ways; but we are not born with the actual possession of knowledge; nor, so far as we can see, is knowledge, at any subsequent time, obtained by us, except by means of the capabilities to which we have referred. We have by nature powers of knowing objects, both external to our organization, and internal; but the objects themselves, and not the representations of them, are presented to us before we know them. We are conscious of seeing, and smelling, and tasting, and feeling, etc.; but they are the things themselves which we see, and smell, and taste, and feel, in the first instance, although afterwards we are able to contemplate the representations of them which are formed in the mind. There is within us, no doubt, a capability of apprehending, p. 8in a sufficient degree, the perfections of God, when they are declared to us; but a knowledge of these perfections does not naturally exist within us. We conclude, then, that, as the Deity is not directly perceived

- 4 -

by us, has not in practice been adequately discerned by any process of the mind, and is not made known to us by any connate, or subsequently implanted idea, we must be indebted to revelation, in the main, for any knowledge we may obtain respecting Him. We do not consider it necessary to enter into a discussion of Pantheistic views, inasmuch as we have yet to learn that Pantheism has ever furnished any definite ideas respecting the nature of God which will bear the test of a close examination as to their reality. We think, too, that it is destructive of the personality of either God, or man, or both, and thus does away with all real relation between the two.

Before proceeding to the investigation of what we mean by a revelation, we will endeavour to answer an objection which may be raised. It may be alleged that, if a true knowledge of God is of such great consequence to man, it appears strange that such differing opinions should have been held on the subject, and that God's revelation—on the supposition that there is one—should not have been more extensively promulgated, and declared with more irresistible evidence. There is no doubt a difficulty here. It does not however attach *especially* to the subject of a revelation; but meets us at all points, when we consider the unequal distribution of the blessings of nature. Why many persons should be destitute of the advantages which others enjoy, and why some should pass a life of suffering, while others are surrounded with every comfort, are questions which naturally arise in the minds of reflecting men, but which p. 9have hitherto remained without full and satisfactory answers. He who would give a complete reply must have clearer views, than have yet been obtained, with regard to the origin of evil. It may be observed too that, on the supposition that the Bible is a real revelation from God, and bearing in mind the vast number of the human race to whom it has already been given, and its capability of future communication, it far more nearly meets the difficulty, than abstruse speculations respecting the Deity, which can scarcely be apprehended even by philosophers, and which are to the mass wholly unintelligible.

2. Let us now examine *the conditions under which a revelation may be expected to be given to the original recipients.*

It may be observed in the first place that a revelation *must possess some distinctive character.* Even, if it should turn out that there is no such thing in reality at all, at least the notion which we form in our minds must possess such points of difference as to distinguish it from all other notions. It appears needful to bear this in mind, obvious though it is, because there are not a few, in the present day, who deprive the word, revelation, of nearly all the distinguishing features which have commonly been supposed to attach to it, and so extend the meaning of the word inspiration as "sometimes to believe it in poets, legislators, philosophers, and others gifted with high genius," (Essays and Reviews, p. 140). What this means it is hard to say. Shakespeare, Milton, Newton, and others certainly did not imagine that they had direct communication with God; that they revealed to us His nature, and the relation in which He stands to us; predicted future events, etc., in the same sense that Moses, David, Isaiah, and the other writers of the Bible are supposed to have done. If they actually did anything of this kind, they were assuredly wholly unconscious of their power; nor, we may add, has common opinion held that they afforded information on the same subjects as those which the writers of the Bible handled. Admirers of our poets, and philosophers, have not considered it necessary to promulgate what they have found in their writings, as matters in which the spiritual, and, possibly, eternal interests of man are vitally concerned; although believers in the Bible, and even in Mahomet, have done so. The word inspiration, in fact, as used in the passage above quoted, involves a confusion of ideas which we should hardly have expected to find in the writings of any one who professed to speak accurately, and appears scarcely pardonable, or even honest, in the case of so acute a thinker, as the late Mr. Baden Powell. We are not now saying that the Bible is a revelation from God, or even that there is such a thing as a distinctive revelation at all. All we assert is, that the idea of such a thing is a very common one, and that it is very different from that which is usually held with regard to the works of Newton, Milton, and other gifted sages and philosophers. We might add, in passing, that, unless the Bible be an imposture—in which case it ought to be regarded as far inferior to the works of genuine and truthful poets and philosophers—it does correspond, as we trust will be seen, on an examination of its contents, to the idea referred to.

Still further, revelation must not only have some distinctive character; but, in order to be effectual for its purpose, *it should carry along with it, to the original recipients, a reasonable conviction of its authenticity.* The Bible speaks of several professed modes of communication, and accepting them according to the ordinary meaning of words, and not in any mythical, or ideological sense, they appear to be such as might answer for the purpose of authentication. The Lord talked with Abraham. He appeared in a burning bush to Moses, spake to him and the children of Israel on Mount Sinai, and conversed with him afterwards on the top of that mountain, during a period of forty days. He spake in the night to Samuel. He appeared in a vision to Isaiah and others. To some He made Himself known in dreams. Christ spake to His disciples. All these are evidently ways in which God might communicate with man; and there is no difficulty in supposing that the attendant circumstances, such for instance as some of those recorded in the Bible, might be of such a kind as to authenticate the communication. It would be idle to argue that, because God does not make Himself known in any of these ways now, He has never done so; for, to omit other considerations, we may observe that, in accordance with the economy which prevails in the works of God, we have no reason to suppose that He would make special revelations to more persons than might be necessary for the purpose He had in view. If He revealed Himself to them, the promulgation of the revelation would be naturally and safely left to more ordinary instrumentality. At the present time, so far as Christians are concerned, they do not expect a special revelation to themselves, because, as they believe, God has already communicated all that He desires them to know.

But supposing a revelation to be sufficiently authenticated,—What may be reasonably expected as to the *extent* of it? It is, we think, clear in the first place that *no perfect knowledge of God and His relation to us could be communicated.* Even if a direct presentation of the Infinite were given, the capacity of man could not grasp it, and therefore the result would be a finite conception; and, if the revelation were made by words or other signs, it is plain that these can only express the finite ideas of which they are the symbols.

Nor is there anything in this which need excite our surprise; for the limited nature of our knowledge with regard to God would be analogous to that which we have about other things. There is nothing with regard to which our knowledge is not limited. Some may be ready to affirm that we do not know things in themselves at all, but only the effects produced upon us, or their relation to us. We are not about to maintain this proposition; but it is at any rate plain that the most familiar objects, as science advances, often disclose to us new qualities, and that we have no reason to suppose that we are fully acquainted with all the qualities of even the simplest substances. There is no reason to expect that the book of revelation should be more explicit than that of nature.

Not only, however, *must* our knowledge, derived from revelation, be, in some degree, limited; but it is not difficult to see, why *it would be probably kept even within the range of what it is possible for us to know.* We can readily understand that the object of God in making a revelation would be to inform us about those things only, a knowledge of which might be essential to our interests; and here again the analogy of the natural world comes in to assist us. God has given to each existence such qualities as are requisite for the position in which it is placed. Ascending through the various classes of animals, we find, as we advance, the capacities for knowledge increasing, and bearing a relation to their actual circumstances. The mole is not endowed with the far-seeing vision which is essential to the well-being of the eagle: nor, on the other hand, has the eagle the power of threading its way through the earth, without which the mole could not exist. Viewing man in relation to the natural world, we find that he has the power of obtaining that kind of knowledge which is necessary to his welfare here, although, in many respects, he is far surpassed by the keener perceptions of the inferior animals. God has in fact ordered and limited his knowledge with an express reference to the position which he is called upon to occupy. This throws light upon the subject of revelation. It is reasonable to expect that God would limit the knowledge communicated in that way also, by a consideration of the state in which man is placed here, and of that which, upon the supposition of a future state, he is to occupy hereafter.

So far as we have yet gone, there does not appear to be any reason why the knowledge, although limited, should not be accurate as far as it goes. Though we do not know all the properties of particular objects, we may know some of them, and may also safely reason about those with which we are acquainted, so long as we are careful not to introduce into the reasoning anything which does not result from our actual knowledge; and so, turning from nature to a revelation, we may learn much from it about God, as for instance, that He is a God of love and holiness; that He will act towards us in a particular manner; that He will punish some actions and recompense others; and this knowledge also may be a true knowledge, so far as it goes, and one that we may safely act upon, although we may still be in ignorance of His exact nature and many points of our relationship to Him.

There is, however, a light in which revelation must be viewed, which involves considerations of a somewhat different character from those hitherto noticed, and to this we now turn. A revelation must not only be limited by the extent of the human capacity for receiving it, and by the proposed object of it, but also, in a considerable degree, by *the state of knowledge existing in the world at the time it is made*. In fact, without some such limitation, it would be unintelligible, and, consequently no revelation. As this truth has frequently been misapplied, we will endeavour to explain, as accurately as we can, our meaning. God could, perhaps, if He thought proper, give in an ignorant age a revelation, as full and explicit, as in a more enlightened period—a revelation we mean which should be understood—but it must be remembered that this could only be effected by altering the conditions under which human knowledge is acquired. For example, to have given a correct theory of the motions of the heavenly bodies, before the age of Newton, would have been impossible, without an entire change both in the existing state of knowledge, and also in the method of acquiring it. Down to the present time all history and experience testify to the fact that the acquisition of knowledge is *gradual*; but such a revelation, as that to which we have referred, would require that it should be made *per saltum*. If knowledge were given in this way the usual course would be completely changed; and not only so, but the knowledge communicated would be altogether out of proportion to that possessed on other points, and would place those who had it in a false and unsatisfactory state with regard to the world in which they lived. To see this we have only to picture to ourselves the condition of a man living in a savage, or only partially civilized state of society, with his mind preternaturally expanded to that of a Newton, and put into possession of the knowledge which he had on some of those subjects which the Bible touches on. How entirely out of harmony would he be with his fellow-men, and everything around him! and, how unable would he be even to pursue his studies for want of those instruments, books, and appliances which a more advanced state of society alone can produce! A revelation of this kind would clearly not be a boon, but an injury to him. It may be observed, moreover, that a revelation, adapted to the knowledge even of a Newton, would neither exactly correspond with facts, nor obviate all the difficulties which a more enlightened age might discover. We do not stop to dwell upon the obvious fact, that such a revelation, as that which we have been noticing, would require not only a preternatural expansion of faculties in the person to whom it was made, but also a similar expansion, or, if not, a long educational process in the case of all those who should receive it. We conclude, then, that a revelation must be adapted to, and in a great degree limited by, the state of knowledge existing in the world at the time when such revelation is made.

This leads us to a consideration of the *necessarily phenomenal character of some portions of a revelation*, respecting which objections against the Bible have been frequently raised. We will, to explain our views, take as an example, the familiar instance of the sun and earth. According to appearance the sun moves, and the earth is stationary: but science has demonstrated that the opposite to this is the real state of the case. What line might it be expected that a revelation would take, when it had to deal with a case of this kind? Should it speak according to appearances, or realities? This, we believe, is the exact point to be considered, and we do not think, when fairly put, that it is one about which there is much difficulty. If a revelation were given to an ignorant people, in accordance with the reality, it is quite clear that they would not be in a condition to receive it, and would therefore, probably, reject it as absurd; but if the description were given according to the appearance presented, then no difficulty would be felt. The question, however, is pressed—whether such a mode of representation is consistent with the truthfulness which may be expected in a revelation.

It might, we think, be a sufficient reply to say that, as, according to our former reasoning, it is, in many cases, the only possible mode of revelation consistent with the established order of things, we may well be content with it; but we will pursue the subject a little further, with the view of making clear how the matter stands. It may be observed that, if absolute truth on a particular subject cannot be communicated, the nearest approximation to it is, not only all that can be expected, but is in itself highly desirable. If a man is unable to receive as full an apprehension of a thing as we have ourselves, we must endeavour to give him the most perfect information which he is capable of receiving. We do not injure him by doing this, but we should injure him if we omitted to do it. If a man, who had lived all his life in the Arctic regions, and had never heard of any other country, were to be brought to England, it would not be necessary to tell him, with a view to his comfort here, the motion of the earth with regard to the sun, and the causes of the length of our days and nights, and of the variation of the seasons. To enter into these matters would confuse his mind, and the man, if he had to earn his living, would starve while he was acquiring the knowledge of them. By such a course of proceeding we should, in reality, do him a great injustice. Instead of attempting anything of the kind, we should naturally give him such information as might be requisite for his practical guidance, in a popular manner, and leave to himself the acquisition of such scientific truth as he might be desirous of becoming acquainted with. In a word, we should describe to him things as they appear to be, and in this respect our description would be, in a certain sense, true; we should not describe them as they really are, and so far our description would not be in strict accordance with the facts of the case. We were about to say that it is a choice of difficulties; but, is there any real difficulty in the case? Does not the common sense of mankind declare that the mode of proceeding which we have described is the only proper one, and that there is no real untruthfulness in it? It may be noticed too that even scientific men continually make use of it amongst themselves, and in their intercourse with others, and this without any charge of untruthfulness being brought against them. What objection then can possibly lie against the adoption of the same method in a revelation? [17] The supposed object of a revelation is to save the soul, or, at least, to advance in a material degree our spiritual interests. Is that to be put aside till the world has learnt scientific truth, and is able to converse in scientific language? We feel no difficulty in leaving the answer to this question to the common sense of mankind in general. We conclude, then, that as phenomenal truth is in many cases the only truth which can possibly be afforded, and the imparting of it is a boon, and not an injury, there is no reason why the Deity should not, when He sees fit, make use of this mode of communication in revelation.

We will now notice, distinctly, *words as a medium of revelation*. It is plain, that in communicating knowledge, they are only effectual by calling up in the mind of the hearer ideas *already* existing. To speak to a man who has been blind from his birth, of colours would be useless, because he has had no experience of them, and consequently no ideas corresponding to them. Words may bring up ideas in a different *combination* from any which had previously existed in the mind of the person spoken to; but they cannot *create* ideas. They may make the hearer acquainted with something which he has never actually perceived; may cause him to reason in a new manner; to see a familiar object in a fresh light, or, in some other way, bring the faculties of the mind into play; but still the mind, so far as instruction by words is concerned, can only act upon its previous stores, and analyze or combine them into new forms. This being the case, it is clear that a revelation, so far as it is made by words, must be limited by the ideas previously existing in the mind of the person to whom it is made. These ideas, too, however numerous and refined they may be, are limited by the experience which a man has had of the external world, and of himself. He cannot get beyond these. If, then, God should think fit to reveal, in words, a knowledge of Himself, or any other object which does not come within the direct cognizance of our perceptive faculties, this can only be effected by calling up in the mind, through the words, some new combination of ideas already possessed. This may not correspond precisely with the object, respecting which the revelation is made; but, as it is the only way in which a revelation by words can be effected, we have no just reason to find fault with it. All we have a right to expect, is that the words should call up in the mind those ideas which best represent the object designed to be revealed.

This may tend to throw some light upon what are called anthropomorphic ideas of God. These have sometimes been spoken of as inadequate, and degrading. Inadequate they certainly are, as every notion which we can have of the Deity must be; but we are unable to see in what way they are degrading. Almost every nation, following apparently the necessity of our nature, has clothed its gods in the objective form of some familiar animal, or other existence, and endowed them with qualities of which they had experience. What wonder then if God, seeing that He must, unless the conditions of our nature were altered, make use of ideas with which we are already familiar, should adopt an anthropomorphic representation of Himself, purified, exalted, and adapted, as far as possible, to His own infinite perfections? In fact, we know not how God could declare Himself as just, righteous, pure, and loving, or reveal our responsibility to Himself, without a reference to man, inasmuch as he is the only being, of which we have any actual experience, who possesses, even in a limited degree, qualities of such a description. Assuredly then it cannot be a degrading notion of the Deity to regard Him as invested with the highest attributes of which we have a conception. We are aware that some philosophers talk much of the Infinite, and the Absolute, as conveying more exalted notions of the Divine Being. What the exact meaning of those terms is philosophers find it difficult to declare, and the common people are almost wholly unable to understand. Certainly such highly abstract terms convey little distinct meaning. It will be found upon examination, that the word "Infinite," to stir in any degree the depths of our nature, must be combined with some quality with which we are familiar. Infinite love, infinite justice, infinite purity, are things which we can in some degree understand and appreciate; but the point which we understand best is not the "Infinite," but the finite,—the love,— the justice,—the purity; and these are ideas taken from what we find in some imperfect degree in ourselves. To those who believe that man was made "in the image of God," and that the Word, being God, became also man, the train of thought here indicated will come home with additional force.

What has been said with regard to a revelation, made by words, applies, in its main points, to a revelation made directly to the mind through *ideas*, without the intervention of words. To see this clearly, let us bear in mind the distinction between a perception and an idea. An idea is the result of a perception. We perceive a rose when it is presented to our senses, and we see, smell, or touch it. We have an idea of it, when, not being any longer presented, we think of it, and call to mind its qualities. We are said to have a perception of anger, or love, or any other emotion, when those feelings are present to the mind. We have ideas of them, when we think about them. It is not our object to enter upon any abstruse discussion as to the origin of ideas. What has been just advanced will be generally admitted by metaphysicians, and readily understood by others. Hoping, then, that the distinction between an idea and a perception will be carried in the mind, we will proceed with our argument. There is no difficulty in supposing—and this, we believe, corresponds very closely to an opinion commonly entertained respecting inspiration—that God could, without the intervention of words, call up in the mind such ideas as He might think fit. For instance, instead of speaking the words, "Thou shalt do no murder," He might, in a preternatural manner, excite in the mind the ideas corresponding to them. Still, however, unless we suppose the conditions of human thought to be altered in a manner for which we have no analogy, the ideas of a man, killing, etc., must previously exist in the mind, or the revelation would be unintelligible. Whether, then, the ideas are called up, through the instrumentality of words, or in some other way, is immaterial to our present argument. The point we insist on is that, except in the case of actual perception, the communication of knowledge, by revelation, or otherwise, *must be limited by the ideas previously existing in the mind of the person to whom the communication is made.* These ideas may be combined into new forms, and new relations may be discovered between them, or they may be analyzed into their constituent parts, but we cannot transcend the ideas themselves, except by new perceptions.

Let it not, however, be imagined that a revelation, conveyed through the instrumentality of ideas previously existing, must be so narrow as to convey little or no new information, or instruction. We have only to look at the works of Milton, Newton, Shakespeare, and other great men, to see the almost endless variety with which ideas, and the relations in which they stand to each other, may be so combined and disposed, as to minister to the imagination, or enrich the mind with fresh stores of knowledge. All the information which we derive from books, or conversation, is obtained in this way, and to it we must probably attribute by far the largest portion of our mental acquisitions, after the period of childhood. So far, indeed, as the promulgation of a revelation by its original recipients is concerned, it appears plain that it must be made, almost necessarily, through the instrumentality of words, inasmuch as they are the best signs which can be made use of in the communication of knowledge.

Before, however, proceeding to this portion of the subject, it appears desirable to make a few additional observations with regard to a revelation by *perception*. We have already had occasion to notice that "the Deity does not, like other objects, come within the direct cognizance of our perceptive faculties" (p. 5), and that, "even if a direct presentation of the Infinite were given . . . the result would be a finite conception" (p. 12). It may, however, be imagined that a direct presentation, even though issuing in a finite conception, or a representation either addressed *ab extra* to our perceptive faculties, or brought before us in a vision, or a dream, or otherwise, would convey to the mind a more correct apprehension of God's nature than could be obtained in any other way. These cases, though differing in some particulars, may, for our present purpose, be regarded as identical, and treated as perceptions. Now there can be no doubt that a perception conveys a more vivid impression to the mind than a description; and we may, therefore, reasonably suppose that, in a revelation, God might use this method of communicating knowledge in those cases to which it might be specially adapted. Thus, for instance, if God designed to give an idea of some place or being which we had never seen, He might effect this, in a very perfect manner, by bringing such a place or being, either in reality, or by representation, within the range of our perceptive faculties. The appearance vouchsafed by God to Moses (Exod. xxxiii. 19–23), the vision of Ezekiel (Ezek. xxxvii. 1–10), and the description given by St. Paul (2 Cor. xii. 1–4), will serve as illustrations of our meaning.

It must not, however, be taken for granted that such a mode of revelation would, in every case, be possible; or that, if possible, it would always be the best method of communication. So far as we can see, no mere presentation, or representation of the Deity, could, in itself, give any deep insight into His moral character, or the relation in which He stands to us. Even if the Deity were constantly present, we know not how we could obtain any accurate knowledge of His attributes, except by observation of His words and acts. If we had been introduced to the philanthropist, Howard, we could not have become acquainted with his excellence by merely gazing at his countenance. We must have listened to his words, and followed him to those scenes of misery which he was in the habit of visiting, if we would obtain a clear understanding of his benevolence. So too, the holiness, love, and other moral perfections of the Deity, are not matters which can be apprehended from any mere intuition of the Divine nature. A glorious exhibition of the Divine presence, such, for instance, as that described in Exodus, as having occurred on Mount Sinai, might inspire feelings of awe, and enable those who witnessed it to apprehend more clearly, perhaps, than could have been effected in any other way, the dignity and majesty of God; but, for a revelation of His moral nature, and the relation in which He stands to man, we must look more to words—such words, for instance, as He is said to have spoken to the children of Israel at that time, and afterwards, during forty days, to Moses. While, then, we think that a revelation by perception, with regard to some things, might be expected, we do not consider that it would convey a large amount of information, unless it were combined with a revelation through words. Words are, in fact, the most natural and effectual mode of imparting most kinds of knowledge, and we may, therefore, reasonably expect that, in any revelation which the Divine Being might think fit to make to man, they would form a chief method of communication. When we thus speak of words in connection with a revelation, we do not mean only words addressed actually to the ear, but also such, as in a dream or vision, may appear to be spoken. We desire also that it should be remembered that, for the main purpose of our argument, it is not so much words as *ideas* which we wish to keep in view. What we chiefly wish to leave on the mind is, that a revelation, except so far as a new perception may be given, *must be limited by the ideas previously existing in the mind of the person to whom it is made.* It may be reasonably expected that God would make use of those ideas which were best adapted to His purpose, but not that He should transcend the ideas themselves. If, too, we suppose that a new perception is given, that perception could not be explained to others, except through the instrumentality of such ideas as those to which we have referred.

Our object hitherto has been to explain the conditions under which a direct revelation from God may be expected to be *given*. If we have been able to remove from the minds of our readers vague and indefinite notions on the subject, and to put, in their place, something clearer and more distinct, our object thus far will have been answered.

It is, perhaps, hardly necessary to state that, by what has been said above, we do not intend to intimate that the recipient of a direct revelation must, necessarily, always understand the exact meaning of such a revelation. It may contain a hidden meaning, to be evident at some future time. Thus, for instance, on the supposition that the first chapter of Ezekiel is a revelation from God, it is probable that the meaning of it was as unintelligible to Ezekiel, as it is generally considered to be at the present time. But the meaning of the words themselves, and their connection with each other are clear. It is in the application that the difficulty arises. So, too, as advances are made in knowledge, words, and the ideas belonging to them, acquire a more extended and fuller meaning. The ideas involved in the word, *sun*, are very different to the philosopher and the peasant; and some ideas contained in a revelation may be of such a kind as not to be fully understood till more knowledge has been acquired, than existed at the time when the revelation was made. But to suppose that the words convey no meaning to the original recipient of the revelation, is to say that no revelation is made to him at all, and it certainly hardly appears probable that the Divine Being should make a communication which could answer no end to the person to whom it was addressed.

3. We now proceed to an examination of the conditions under which *a revelation may be recorded, or otherwise made known by the person who has received it*. Here we see at once that, for all practical purposes, the method of communication must be *words*; for it is not necessary to take into account such visual representations as might be made to the eye by painting or otherwise. Words may be oral, or written. As the latter are more likely to be well weighed and definite than the former, and are, moreover, better calculated to hand down a truth from age to age, we shall confine our attention to them, although what we have to say is, in a great degree, applicable to spoken words also. We start with the supposition that God has already made known to some particular person, as perfectly as He has thought fit, and, it may be, as perfectly as the nature of the subject admitted, or the capability of the person to whom the communication has been made would allow, some truth which is to be recorded for the benefit of the present, and future generations. The question we have to answer is,—how this may be most effectually accomplished.

It is obvious that, in the case of a revelation, made by words, *the words might be recorded exactly as they were delivered*. The words which God is said to have spoken on Mount Sinai, and to have written afterwards, on two tables of stone, may serve as an exemplification of our meaning. In this case God is described as writing them with His own hand: but they might have been written, with equal truthfulness, by any of those who had heard them. If future generations had convincing evidence that they possessed a faithful record of what God said, and the meaning of the words had not changed during the lapse of time, the revelation would be as perfect to them as it was to the original recipients. So, too, if God, instead of speaking the words of the ten commandments, had, in some way which should authenticate the reality of the revelation, called up in the mind of Moses the ideas corresponding to the words, and he had faithfully written them down; those words would convey as full a revelation to those who read them, as that which Moses himself had experienced. Both these would be verbal revelations in the strict sense of the word. They would be, in fact, the very words of God Himself. If any book, professing to be a revelation from God, could be proved to be entirely of this description, there would be little or no room for discussion about it. The only things which could give rise to dispute would be such as attach to the interpretation of all records. Questions might be asked as to the exact meaning of the words, and inquiries might be raised as to whether they retained the same meaning which they had when they were originally written down: but any dispute which might arise on these points would be confined within very narrow limits, and would moreover be of such a character, as could not be avoided, unless God were to make a revelation afresh in every age, and we may add, perhaps, to every individual,—a supposition which would be contrary to analogy, and in the highest degree improbable. Thus far there is no practical difficulty.

Is it, however, necessary to the idea of a recorded revelation that the exact words, neither *more nor less*, as spoken by God, or as expressing ideas which He has called up in the mind of the person to whom He has revealed Himself, should be written down? A recorded revelation, we must remember, is designed chiefly for the benefit of future generations, and it may therefore very properly leave out much which was only of passing interest. God might have revealed many things to Abraham, which were highly important for him to know, but in which we may have no interest. We can easily see then that, in any record which God might authorize, such things would very probably be omitted. Thus far again there is no practical difficulty.

To proceed a step further. Is there any reason to expect that, in a record of a revelation, the original words, either as spoken by God, or as expressive of the ideas which He had called up in the mind of the recipient, might be in any decree *altered?*—and, would every alteration necessarily make the record less a revelation from God than it was before? These are questions which we shall endeavour to answer.

It may be observed, in the first place, that the same train of thought which applies to an original revelation from God, applies also, in its main points, to the record of it. Both in the one case, and the other, it appears reasonable to expect that God would not, to a greater extent than was absolutely necessary, transcend or interfere with those natural powers in man which He had Himself implanted. As the giving of a revelation would, as already shewn, be conformed in a great degree to the usual conditions under which knowledge is imparted, so also, it seems reasonable to expect that the record of a revelation would as far as possible be conformed to the usual conditions under which knowledge is recorded.

In looking at the conditions under which a revelation must be recorded, it is obvious that the difference of languages, which prevails in this world, presents an insuperable obstacle to an exact record of words being continued. It may indeed be alleged that God could cause a revelation to be recorded, in its exact words, in each distinct language. We hardly think however that such a view as this will be seriously entertained by any one. Not to mention how completely contrary this would be to what analogy would lead us to expect, we may observe that, as languages are continually undergoing changes, such a method of recording must be continually renewed; and, moreover, as language does not convey precisely the same ideas to any two individuals, it would be almost needful that a separate record, or rather a separate revelation, should be made for each person. Such views as these require only to be stated to shew that they are untenable; but, if they are untenable, it is plain that the *continuance* of an exact record of words cannot be expected.

But may it not be expected that, at least, *one* exact record would be made of any revelation which God might think fit to give, and that this would afford the best guarantee which could be had for future truthfulness? In answering this question it is very important to draw a distinction. *The words of the record may be exactly such words as God approves of, although they may not be the precise words in which the original revelation was made.* In some particular instances God might determine that the precise words of the revelation should be used, while in others He might think fit that it should be otherwise. In either case the record would be a true one, and each method of recording might have its own peculiar advantages. Under some circumstances it might be desirable that not the slightest deviation from the precise mode of expression which God had communicated should be made; while under others, the human view—by which we here mean the view of the particular person to whom the revelation is made—might be recorded, and add to it a force which could hardly be had in any other way. So long as the record is such as God approves of, every requisite to a true record is complied with. If a minister of state were commissioned to make a communication to a foreign court, he might write down the whole or a part of it in his own words, and, if his own court approved of the words, contained in the writing, the object in view would be answered. We can even understand that, in some respects, the communication might gain force by this mode of proceeding. The ηθος of the writer would be manifested, and carry with it a certain degree of weight. There would be the weight which attached to the document as emanating from the government, and there might be an additional weight from the character of the person who had been entrusted to write, and, perhaps, carry out, in some degree, the requirements of, the dispatch. In the case of a recorded revelation, it appears then probable that God would permit those feelings and powers which He has implanted in man, and which exert such a strong influence on others, to do their work, subject, however, to His own control and guidance. In this way there would be a Divine and a human aspect of the record; a Divine and a human power in it. All of it would be the truth of God, and it would be presented to us in a manner peculiarly adapted to our condition, and likely to ensure our acceptance of it. At the very least such a method of recording would be exactly consistent with truthfulness.

We may go a step further, and say that it would be difficult, if not impossible, to conceive any circumstances under which the record should not bear a human aspect. If the views propounded in the former part of these "Thoughts," with regard to the conditions under which a revelation must be made, and especially with respect to anthropomorphic views of God, be correct, a revelation *must* assume, in some measure, a human aspect. But if the human aspect must exist in the presentation, it must also in the record. The only question which is really open to discussion is, whether there should be the *same* human aspect in the record, as in the original revelation; in other words, whether it may be expected that God would always present that particular human aspect in the original revelation which He considered best adapted for the record. For the reasons already assigned it does not seem probable that this would be the case.

It must be remembered, moreover, that in the case of a revelation, made at different times, and to different persons, either the character of each individual writer must be manifested in the record, or some other character, alien perhaps to that of the writer, and certainly not equally adapted to that of all the readers, must be adopted. Which method of record appears the most probable, and the most calculated to promote the object of a revelation—namely, to instruct and influence mankind—it does not appear very difficult to determine. It seems, then, that a variety of style may be expected in the records written by different persons of the revelations which they have received. As has been before observed, all that is essential to the truthfulness of the record is that God should approve of it.

A question may possibly arise here as to the precise *manner* in which the words may be so recorded, as to convey a true account of God's revelation. In endeavouring to supply an answer, it should be remembered, in the first place, that in the ordinary affairs of life no great difficulty occurs with regard to the transmission of a message. If the person who has been selected to convey it, has sufficient intelligence to understand it, and is, moreover, desirous to deliver it faithfully, he is, in most cases, able either to speak, or write it, in his own words, in such a manner as to convey the right meaning to others. So, too, with regard to a revelation; if the person to whom it has been made rightly apprehends it, and endeavours to record it honestly, the probability is great that the record which he makes will be a true one. If, too, we are prepared, in accordance with the common belief in all ages, to admit that God can, and at times does, exercise a control over the minds of men, it is reasonable to believe that He would do this, when the object was to furnish a correct record for the benefit of future ages. This control might be exercised either consciously, or unconsciously to the writer. All that would be needful for the truthfulness of the record is, that it should be exercised in some way.

4. We will now proceed to offer some remarks as to the conditions under which *a revelation may be expected to be transmitted.* Much of what has been said, with regard to the recording of a revelation, by the person to whom it was originally made, applies to the transmission of such a record to future generations, and its translation into other languages. If a belief (in what way originated we do not now stop to enquire) in the reality of the recorded revelation existed, the greatest care would naturally be taken in making copies from it, and also in translating it. Well-known examples of this are to be found in the care which the Jews of old used in making new copies of their sacred books, and also in the fact that, in our own country, no printers, but those appointed by the Queen, are permitted to publish the authorized version of the Bible. It can hardly be considered possible that those who believed in the reality of a recorded revelation, and valued it, would not take care to hand it down in a correct form to others; and, although incorrect, mutilated, and interpolated copies, might, in some instances, be made by other persons, it does not seem likely that these would prevail to such an extent, as to prevent the true record from maintaining its ground. Such dishonest copies would hardly be made at all, till considerable interest had been manifested in the revelation; and *then* any variations from the correct copies would scarcely pass without challenge, and correction.

It appears then, that, as the ordinary mode of recording, copying, and translating important communications are usually found sufficiently adequate for their several purposes, such methods might be employed with success in regard to a revelation: and it also seems probable that God would not interfere with such methods more than was absolutely necessary for the purpose He had in view. If we suppose that God exercised, throughout the whole process of transmission, that controlling power to which reference has been made; then there would be a correct record in each age. That God should exercise that power to such an extent as to prevent every possibility of error, in the transmission of the record, or of mistake as to its meaning in the minds of those who read it, would be contrary to the analogy of His dealings with us in other things. We possess faculties, by the due exercise of which we are enabled to arrive at a sufficiently accurate knowledge of those things which are essential to our wellbeing, but we are not, by infallible guidance, preserved from error. If we were, our responsibility would to a great extent cease. All that can be reasonably expected, in the case under consideration, is that the record should be transmitted with such exactness, as that an honest inquirer should be able to ascertain its authenticity, and understand its meaning, so far as God designed that he should know it. We say—so far as God designed that he should know it,—because it is quite conceivable that there might be mysteries in a revelation, the meaning of which would not be made clear till the time determined beforehand by God should arrive.

5. To enter into a full examination, as to what would constitute sufficient grounds for *accepting* a professed revelation, would open too wide a field of enquiry for our present purpose, and would necessitate a discussion of that very difficult branch of metaphysics which relates to the laws which regulate our belief. Without, however, attempting to discuss the subject fully, a few points may be indicated for consideration.

It is clear that the evidence, with regard to the record of a professed revelation, *will vary in its character at different times.* The evidence will be more direct, and, in this respect, more clear, at an earlier period of the record, than at a later: while, on the other hand, a record which has been translated into different languages, and has exercised a widely spread influence, will possess a peculiar force of its own. On the supposition that God made a revelation to Moses, it is not difficult to suppose that convincing evidence, as to the truthfulness of what he might say, or write about it, might readily be afforded to those who lived in his times. If such miracles, as those recorded in the Pentateuch really occurred—and certainly if God so far transcended the usual course of nature as to give a revelation, it does not seem hard to believe that He might also so far transcend it, as to authenticate it in some special manner—the evidence would be of a very strong kind. To say, however, that no reasonable conviction of the reality of a revelation could be afforded, without the aid of miracles, is an assertion which we are not prepared to hazard; though we certainly think that, as calculated to excite attention, and implying a power superior to that of man, they would serve as excellent credentials. To human view, in fact, a miracle does not necessarily imply the agency of the one God. It might, for anything that can be proved to the contrary, be the work of some power, inferior to that God whom we are bound to obey, and yet superior to man. The various circumstances therefore, connected with the miracle, would be properly taken into account by the person who was investigating a professed revelation. He would not only examine with care the evidence as to the reality of the miracle itself, but also the circumstances under which it was worked, and its aspect. The character of the person who professed to have received the revelation would very fairly come under consideration. Inquiries would be made as to whether he was one whose word could be safely trusted, and whether he possessed sufficient intelligence, to render it probable that he would arrive at a right conclusion. A man of known truthfulness and intelligence would justly meet with more ready credence, than a person of an opposite character.

The revelation itself, too, would be closely scrutinized. In some cases it is conceivable that the revelation would go far to prove itself. It might make known things which, though not perhaps discoverable by man's reason, were nevertheless so agreeable to it, as to carry with them an almost irresistible conviction. As, too, a revelation would be given for the practical guidance of man, it would probably be attended with threatenings and promises, or other predictions; and when the things which had been foretold actually took place, the reality of the revelation would be, to a great extent, established. If, for instance, the remarkable occurrences which Moses, on various occasions, foretold, as about to take place in the land of Egypt, really occurred, it would, we think, be very difficult to avoid the conclusion that he had received a revelation from God, and that what he said, or wrote, was to be depended upon. A candid inquirer would also examine, in a reverent spirit, whether the professed revelation was likely to promote a pure morality, and to further the best interests of mankind. He would not, indeed, enter upon such an examination, with the feeling that he was competent to decide, in *every* respect, as to the justice and excellence of the statements which professed to be revealed; for his reason, if consulted, would tell him that many circumstances might be hidden from him, without which a correct judgment could not be formed, and that, possibly, his capacity might not be able to grasp them in all their relations, even if they were put before him. Still, such an examination as that which we have just referred to, would properly form an element in leading to a conclusion, and, when combined with others, would give as reasonable grounds for arriving at a decision with respect to a professed revelation, as we should be willing to act on in the usual business of life, and would, therefore, be suited to the conditions of our being. The decision arrived at would commonly be the result, not of a single proof, but of many concurrent circumstances.

What has been said in reference to an examination, instituted by persons living at the time when a professed revelation was made, is obviously applicable, in many respects, to those who should live in later times, and also to the original recipients themselves. With regard to evidence in later times, it may be added that the original believers in the record, and their followers in each succeeding age, would naturally be subjected to an examination, as to their truthfulness and intelligence, and thus a chain of evidence would be continually kept up. The larger, too, the number, and the more intelligent the character of those who believed in it, the greater would be the presumption in its favour. If the record were received generally by any nation, the *onus probandi* would in that case lie with those who impugned it. The record itself also would, from time to time, be submitted to such fair rules of criticism as apply to other documents, the fact however being remembered, that it professed to be the word of God, and, therefore, that evidence of its authenticity, rather than of its exact coincidence with human reason, was to be mainly looked for.

We have now indicated, although very briefly and imperfectly, a few points for consideration, as to the transmission of a recorded revelation, and what might constitute sufficient grounds for accepting it as true; and we trust that what has been said will suffice to show that there would be no great difficulty in so handing it down, as that it should convey to the candid inquirer, in each succeeding age, reasonable evidence of its reality.

It may, however, be argued, that, although such evidence, as has been indicated, might well convince those who had time and ability to institute a searching examination, the case is different with regard to others; and that, as a revelation may be presumed to have a most important bearing upon the interests of all, there should be some more easy method by which it may be tested. Now, we are quite prepared to admit that every one should have sufficient grounds afforded him for arriving at a decision; but, at the same time, we do not conceive that a thorough examination of the evidence, made by each person for himself, is the only, or even principal, method by which a safe conclusion may be reached. Each individual has commonly some peculiar talent, in the exercise of which he reaches an excellence, which others, whose abilities and pursuits are of a different character, do not attain to. The astronomer works out conclusions, which, those, whose attention has been directed to other subjects, could never have reached, but which they may nevertheless, with propriety, accept as true. It is not every one who has time or ability to sift evidence on theological subjects, or to criticise manuscripts; but the labours of those who have given their attention to such things may, it is evident, justly be available for the benefit of others. Even the wisest person accepts as true much on the testimony of others, and that often on subjects with which he is conversant. When his judgment is most independent he will find, if he analyzes it, that much is borrowed. There is nothing contrary to sound reason in all this. Without it, little progress could be made in anything. Without it, each succeeding age, instead of standing on the platform which had been raised by that which preceded it, would have the weary task of commencing afresh, and could thus make few accessions to knowledge. Trustfulness is as much a part of man's constitution, as reasoning or any other intellectual process. Should it be said that men often trust wrongly; it may be replied with equal force that they as frequently reason wrongly. Probably there is less difficulty in ascertaining where we may safely trust, than in weighing evidence properly, or carrying out correctly a train of reasoning. Certainly people have little difficulty, if they use their faculties aright, in selecting a fit adviser in law or medicine. Why should there be a greater difficulty with regard to religion? We do not mean that anyone would be justified in so placing himself under the guidance of another, as to *give up* the exercise of his own judgment altogether; but, that he may properly make use of the counsel of others, and that often to such an extent as to overrule his own views in *forming* his judgment.

There is another consideration, connected with this portion of the subject, which well deserves attention. A conclusion may be a very correct one, and may have been reached by a very satisfactory process, although the person who has made it, may be unable to state the grounds upon which it rests, or meet the objections which may be made against it. This applies not only to those cases, where the conclusion mainly rests upon trust, but also to others. An eminent statesman recommended a person going out in an official capacity, to give his decisions confidently, but not to venture to declare the reasons. The decisions would probably be right, but the reasons, as *stated by him*, might not be. It need not be inferred from this that the reasons upon which he would really act were wrong, but rather that from want of practice, or power of analysis, or some other cause, he would be unable to bring them out correctly. The processes of thought pass so rapidly through the mind, that even the most practised thinkers often find it difficult to arrest them in their progress, and state the various steps by which they have arrived at their conclusions. The simplest and most certain grounds of our conclusions are, in fact, not unfrequently those which it is most difficult to bring out into distinct view. They have so often passed through the mind that we have ceased to notice them, although, all the while, they contribute essentially to the judgment which is formed; or they lie so far back, in the depths of our consciousness, that it is almost impossible to recover them. Necessarily, nothing can be so simple, or so certain, in one sense, as intuitions, that is, those things which we know or believe without any intermediate process of thought, and yet, down to the present time, those who have most deeply studied the subject hesitate to decide exactly as to what are intuitions, and what are not. We conclude then that, while, on the one hand, we should not discredit the rational powers of men, as if they were unequal to perform the task allotted to them; we must not, on the other, be easily shaken with regard to conclusions which have been made with care and consideration, because we may be unable to trace out accurately the arguments by which they are supported, or answer the objections which are made against them.

We have now considered revelation with regard to the conditions under which it may be expected to be *given*, *recorded*, and *transmitted*, with a view to its being *accepted and believed*. We do not for a moment suppose that we have removed every difficulty; but if we have upon the whole, made clear to our readers the nature of these conditions, or, where this has not been done, indicated the points at which difficulties exist, our chief purpose will have been answered.

6. Here we might leave the subject, but we cannot forbear adding some further observations in reference to that professed revelation of God's will which is to be found in the Bible. It is not our intention to attempt a summary of the various evidences which exist to show that it is a real one; nor is it our design to reply at length to the objections which have been made to invalidate it. There are however some obvious facts which meet us on the threshold of the inquiry, and which can be estimated at their just value by any candid inquirer, to which we would direct attention.

We find for instance that the Bible contains a purer system of morality, and conveys a clearer insight into the unity and nature of God, than is to be found in any other book; and that, although it is the composition of men, many of them ignorant and unlearned, who have lived at different times, and occupied very dissimilar positions in life, there is, nevertheless, a wonderful similarity in the main outlines of religious truth, as delivered by all the writers. We know, however, still further, that the morality and precepts of the Bible, although confessedly of a pure and holy character, are, nevertheless, not of such a kind as to fall in with the wishes and passions of mankind. To believe that morality must extend to thoughts as well as actions, and that an all-seeing God notices, and will one day call all men to a strict account, is not a matter which, if we may judge from what we see around us, is agreeable to the feelings of most men. Nor, if we look to the great remedy proposed for the sin of man, such, we mean, as it is supposed to be, by the great majority of professing Christians, namely, the atoning sacrifice made by the Son of God, do we find here again a matter which either the reason or the feelings of men generally are ready to lead them to adopt. We see too, that in all ages unbelief has, more or less, existed, and objections have been, from time to time, brought forward which appeared likely to have considerable power in undermining the existing belief in the Bible. Persecution also has exercised its influence, and, it might frequently have been supposed, according to human calculations, that it would have availed to destroy all credence in it. And yet, notwithstanding all these circumstances, to which we have referred, it is an incontrovertible fact that a professed belief in the Bible, as a revelation from God, exists most widely. It is, we may add, not a little worthy of being remarked that the nomenclature of the Bible has obtained such a strong hold on the public mind, in our own day, that many who deny inspiration in any distinctive sense, still retain the use of this and other words, as if afraid to make it plain how far they differ from those opinions which are commonly received.

The present age is certainly more enlightened than any which has preceded it; but, hitherto at least, a professed belief in the orthodox doctrines of religion has increased rather than diminished. We find moreover that persons of all ranks, and every kind of mental calibre, have declared that they find something in the Bible which they do not find in any other book; something, in fact, which, when duly received, comes home to their hearts as men, and seems admirably adapted to the deepest wants of human nature. We see too that those who appear to have accepted the Bible most fully, and to hold it most firmly, have been so much impressed with a sense of its importance to the world at large, as to have endeavoured, often at considerable risk and expense, to communicate to others, both at-home and abroad, the knowledge of those things which they have received as truths— a method of proceeding which has not been adopted, and, in fact, could not have been, without a manifest absurdity, by those who profess to believe in the inspiration of Plato, Milton, Shakespeare, and other great, but, according to common opinion, uninspired men. All these and various other considerations which might be adduced seem to mark out the Bible, as being a book at least *different* from all other books, and to lead to the presumption that it may contain that knowledge of God which, as has been remarked in the earlier part of these "Thoughts," it appears most important for men to be acquainted with, and a revelation of which, in some way or other, has been very commonly believed in. Assuredly there is a strong presumption in its favour, and the *onus probandi*, in our own day, lies with those who deny its claims to acceptance. Whether however the Bible actually is, or contains a revelation from God is still a fair subject for reverent examination.

Without attempting to enter upon such an examination here, we may, without impropriety, offer a suggestion as to the *spirit* in which it should be conducted. It must be remembered that the examination of a theological, or any other subject which bears upon the interests of our daily lives, involves principles of a very different character from those which are connected with an investigation of the science of number, or any other abstract science. Mathematical and numerical investigations advance from principles which are clearly defined, and almost universally acknowledged to be self-evident; the reasoning also is of such a kind as to preclude the admission of error. In theology the case is different. There, it is difficult to define with accuracy the points from which the reasoning commences, and also to exclude, with certainty, the possibility of error in the reasoning itself. There is, too, another essential difference between abstract sciences and other subjects of inquiry. It is not only self-evident that two straight lines cannot enclose a space, but the judgment which the mind gives on the subject is not in any danger of being disturbed by the feelings. In theology, however, the matters which come under consideration are so mixed up with our nearest and dearest interests, that the feelings are called into play at every step of the investigation, and a just balance of the judgment cannot be preserved without the exercise of much care. Hence the necessity of endeavouring to preserve a candid and unruffled spirit in all enquiries connected with religion. No doubt those feelings which a beneficent God has implanted with a view to assist us in deciding, are to have their due weight; but certainly there is need of caution, lest they influence us unduly. If the judge thinks it needful to charge the jury to dismiss from their minds everything which might tend to influence their judgments in an improper manner, and attend only to the evidence, even though the matter about which they have to decide is usually one in which they have no personal interest; it certainly does not appear unnecessary to give a similar caution on a subject, with regard to which feeling has assumed so strong a form as to give rise to the name, *odium theologicum*. We deceive ourselves, if we imagine that we approach the subject without any danger of judging it unfairly. This caution, undoubtedly applies to *all* who discuss theological questions; but we think that we shall not be making an unwarranted assertion, if we say that it applies in a special manner to those who *impugn* the Bible revelation, when it is remembered that the doctrines contained in it, as they have generally been received by those who are called orthodox Christians, are of such a kind as very commonly to excite, in the first instance at least, a strong feeling of opposition. The Bible itself intimates this, and common experience bears witness to it as being a fact. We are not now saying that the doctrines of the purity and holiness of God, the dreadful nature of sin, the need of an atonement, the inability of man to present himself before God in merits of his own, and others of a similar kind are true; but we may properly say that, whether true or false, they are such as frequently raise a strong feeling of opposition; and therefore that those who examine them, with the view of ascertaining their character, stand in *special* need of the caution to preserve a calm and candid spirit.

It will not be out of place to introduce here another consideration which has a bearing upon this part of the subject, namely, the *supernatural aid* which the Bible offers towards the understanding and acceptance of its doctrines. It is quite conceivable that a state of things might exist in which such aid would be wholly unnecessary. We might suppose a case in which the nature of man was so entirely in harmony with itself, and so exactly attuned to the truths of a Divine revelation, as readily to accept it, when it was presented; but the question we have to decide is, whether man's nature is actually in this state or not. Observation leads us to believe that it is not. Whether we accept the scripture statement of the fall or not, we must not shut our eyes to the fact that it is difficult for virtue to force its way, while vice has many votaries. However convincing, abstractedly, the reasons may be to enforce the claims of virtue, it is evident that they possess but little power to lead the large majority of mankind. History and experience testify to this. Scarce any deny the evidence in favour of virtue, although few are content to be governed by it. Now it may be fairly presumed that any revelation which the Divine Being might make would be in the interests of virtue; it may be reasonably expected too that it would be supported by strong evidence: but, if, as actual observation makes it clear is the case, the feelings of mankind are more inclined to reject than accept the claims of virtue, the evidence, however strong, will not produce the effect which it would, if the mind were more justly balanced, and thus the revelation will be in danger of being rejected. Such rejection, be it remembered, need not result from any deficiency of evidence, but may arise from an indisposition to receive it. For our own part we believe that the evidence in favour of the orthodox views of scripture statements is far stronger than can be found in support of any other subject of a like kind: but, at the same time, taking into consideration the actual tendencies of human nature, we are not surprised that it does not produce the effect which it should do; and therefore it appears to us not unreasonable to suppose that God might exercise some such supernatural power upon the mind, as the Bible speaks of, with the view of disposing it to the reception of a revelation.

That God does at times interfere in a manner, out of the usual course of His Providence, with regard to other matters, especially in answer to prayer, is believed almost universally. We cannot enter here into a discussion as to the foundation of the belief; but, certainly so long as the records of mankind go back, and so far as the experience of the present day conducts us, the belief has been entertained, and prayer seems to be the natural expression of man's heart in all cases of difficulty. Men *will* believe in, and appeal to, a supernatural power, and it is hard to suppose that a tendency so universal and deeply seated, should have no solid foundation. But if prayer, for aid and direction from above, is the natural outpouring of man's heart with regard to the more ordinary affairs of life, there appears to be no reason why prayer should not be offered up for counsel and guidance with regard to a professed revelation, and that an answer should be expected. At least, it can hardly be said that those have fairly tested the claims of scripture to be received as a revelation from God, who have not complied with the conditions which it has laid down as to the manner in which it should be studied.

We now leave the subject, drawing the attention of our readers to the prayer of one of our greatest poets, and earnestly hoping that his prayer may be theirs:—

     . . . What in me is dark,
     Illumine; what is low, raise and support;

That to the height of this great argument
I may assert Eternal Providence,
And justify the ways of God to man.

Paradise Lost.

FOOTNOTES:

[17] On the subject of the Mosaic cosmogony, see a very interesting Letter from Sir Isaac Newton to Dr. Thomas Burnet, in Sir David Brewster's "Life of Newton," pp. 450–453.

Milton Keynes UK
Ingram Content Group UK Ltd.
UKHW031050120324
439302UK00006B/419

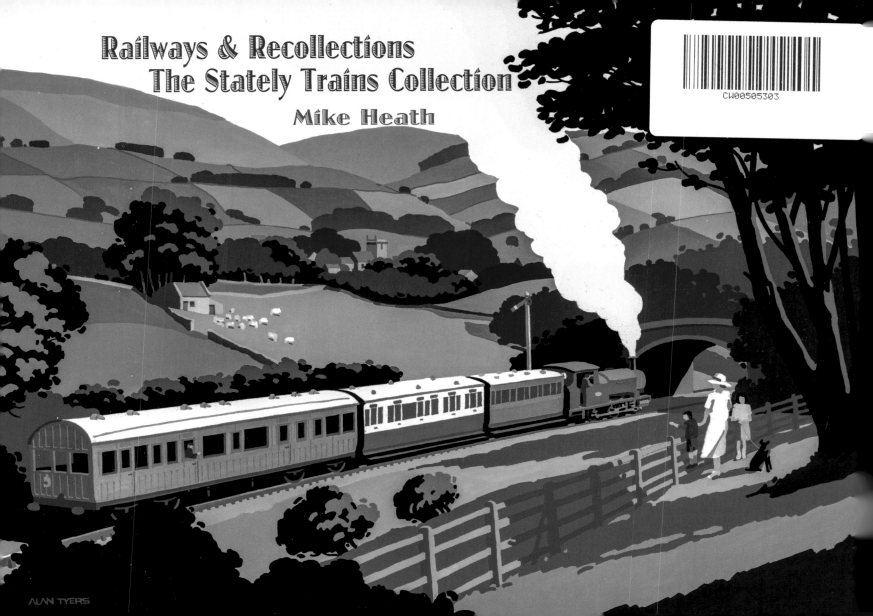

Railways & Recollections
The Stately Trains Collection
Mike Heath

ALAN TYERS

First published in 2021

British Library Cataloguing in Publication Data

A catalogue record for this book is available from the British Library.

ISBN 978 1 85794 575 1

Silver Link Books
Mortons Media Group Limited
Media Centre
Morton Way
Horncastle
LN9 6JR
Tel/Fax: 01507 529535

email: sohara@mortons.co.uk
Website: www.nostalgiacollection.com

Printed and bound in the Czech Republic

Frontispiece: Artwork by Alan Tyers.
Stephen Middleton Collection

Contents

Acknowledgement

While Stephen is the driving force behind 'Stately Trains', it is clear that the impressive restorations described in this book could not be achieved without the active involvement of others, a point Stephen is keen to acknowledge:

'I am extremely grateful to all those who have given assistance with information, parts, labour and encouragement over the years, passengers whose custom will allow these coaches to run well into their second century and, above all, a very understanding and supportive wife.'

Stephen Middleton

The Heritage Railway Carriage database reveals that around 400 of the 5,500 carriages 'preserved' are more than 100 years old, and highlights just how many Victorian and Edwardian carriages are under threat of decaying out of existence.

Most heritage railways operate common former British Railways carriages from the 1950s and '60s. Meanwhile many also own much older, historically significant wooden-bodied railway carriages that, due to a lack of covered storage space, are kept in the open, susceptible to the elements, where they sit rotting gently away. Those railways that have restored such carriages then have to fund accommodation and may only want to use them occasionally to keep them in pristine condition. This means that such carriages are unlikely to repay the time and money spent in restoration. Some railways feel therefore that they have no option other than to scrap unrestored coaches, despite their historical interest. They take up valuable space, make the area look untidy, and there is no one willing to take on such liabilities. The database shows that the numbers of carriages 'available' outstrips demand, so what is to become of the rotting historic examples?

Conventional wisdom suggests that wooden carriages can cost up to £100,000 and ten years to restore. Grant-aiding such work may lead to storage and use restrictions as well as dictate restoration methods. Grants from the lottery and PRISM (The Preservation of Industrial and Scientific Material) are wonderful, but the headline-grabbing '£50,000 awarded to restore a carriage' may deter other carriage owners from even starting work, fearing that their particular project is beyond their financial means.

This is where Stephen Middleton's pragmatic approach to restoration comes in, cutting time and expenditure and creating a good life for the carriage. The reduced time and money spent on restoration together with the profitable use of the completed carriages yields funds available for continued maintenance and to the commencement of the restoration of more 'at risk' carriages. Works may or may not be to approved museum techniques and total authenticity is compromised to suit 21st-century taste and function. However, most museums are sadly unable to accept more artefacts of that size, so it is up to individuals like Stephen to use cost-effective methods to reduce the long lists of 'at risk' carriages so starkly described in the carriage register.

This academic argument, which has been backed up by the success of Stately Trains, may not appeal to the 'traditionalists', but how many of the historic carriages in their collection would have been saved otherwise?

During his first restoration project Stephen was pleased to have received the help, advice and some components from the Midland Railway Centre, which runs its own vintage train of former Midland Railway stock. The MRC's Lee Sharpe and Stephen discussed how they could encourage other

Great Eastern Railway Saloon No 37 in Blackwell Goods Yard on 20 June 1964.
Stephen Middleton Collection, J. Watling

Fifty-five years later, No 37 undergoes further refurbishment and lining out in the works at Embsay in December 2019. *Author*

restorers, who thus far had operated in relative isolation, to share the benefits of this mutual attitude. To this end a 'Carriage Restorers' Convention' was organised with the aim of giving participants the opportunity to share expertise and swap notes in a relaxed and friendly environment. It would also allow 'spare' carriage parts to be offered free, for sale or by exchange, relieving restorers of the need to go to the expense of making them. Stephen hosted the first event, which was held at the Embsay & Bolton Abbey Steam Railway in October 2000. Representatives from the carriage and wagon departments of 34 heritage railways and museums attended and over the past 20 years bodies such as the Bluebell Railway, Isle of Wight Railway, the Scottish Railway Preservation Society, Vintage Carriages Trust, National Railway Museum and many more have hosted what immediately became an annual event. The 'Convention', which returned to Embsay in 2020, combines networking, training, skills demonstrations, health, safety and operational matters, as well as giving attendees the opportunity to see and ride on the host railway's vintage carriages.

It has seen complete unrestored full-size carriages find new homes where they have been restored, and the market for such carriages has opened up and attracted more people to get involved in the restoration, maintenance and operation of fine vintage coaches.

Stephen Middleton was born into a railway family (his father worked for the LNER and BR, his grandfather for the NER, LNER and BR at Ipswich, and his maternal grandfather for the GNR, LNER and BR). With his father holding a 1st Class pass, as a child he enjoyed privileged travel in Pullman cars on the East Coast Main Line in the early 1960s. Impressed by the grandeur of those carriages, dating from the 1920s, and enjoying the refined service offered by the stewards, his boyhood dream was to work on the Pullmans. However, parental encouragement directed him towards a management career and as the railways changed he had no ambition to follow in the footsteps of his father and grandfathers. He did, however, retain a dream of restoring a fine old carriage.

His first attempt was around 30 years ago, when he offered to buy two North Eastern Railway carriage bodies that he had seen on a Harrogate farm, but the farmer refused the sale as his chickens would become homeless. (The carriage bodies eventually fell apart and recently Stephen salvaged parts for the restoration of another coach.)

In November 1992 the Rutland Railway Museum, as it was then known, advertised a 'clearance sale' that aroused his interest, as it included among the items a Great Eastern Railway saloon built in 1889. A visit to inspect the relic revealed a shabby-looking framework piled to the dipping roof with chairs and light fittings. There was no doubt that it had suffered. Nevertheless, he was spurred on by the fact that his family knew this carriage well as it had been based at Ipswich for use by the District Engineer. (His grandfather was Station Master at Ipswich in the 1940s-'50s and his father's boss was the District Engineer when he joined that department in the 1940s.)

While waiting to see if his submitted bid was acceptable, he sought advice on the process of carriage restoration. A visit to see Michael Cope at the Vintage Carriages Trust, based on the Keighley & Worth Valley Railway, was arranged. Following examination of Stephen's photographs of his prospective purchase, Michael took a sharp intake of breath and said, 'Well, of course, with money and time, nothing is impossible.' This meeting gave Stephen useful contacts for parts and expertise and was his introduction to the kind cooperation that he has enjoyed from many people on many railways ever since.

The bid for the Great Eastern Railway carriage No 14 was successful and the purchase was completed in 1993, after which all components were transported to a barn on a farm near Harrogate for restoration.

Above right: In August 1964, at the age of seven, a very content Stephen was photographed on a train heading to Garsdale for a stay at a family cottage at Howgill.

Right: GER No 14 in the 'Home Siding' at Ipswich by the tunnel mouth. This would have been a familiar sight to Stephen's father and grandparents during their working career.
Stephen Middleton Collection, Ken Leighton

The first of these two photographs was taken on 1 July 1998 when, utilising the newly restored GER No 14 carriage, Stephen proudly presented the first 'Strawberry Special' on the Embsay & Bolton Abbey Steam Railway. The second photograph was taken 20 years later at the launch of Queen Victoria's Golden Jubilee Saloon. The intervening years have seen the creation of the Stately Trains collection, which includes eight pre-1914 carriages, some with royal connections, and a 1916-built Hudswell Clarke steam locomotive. Added to this is the unique 1903 North Eastern Railway petrol-electric Autocar and trailer, which, although not part of the Stately Trains stable, is from the same era and was bought by Stephen, who established a charitable trust to restore it. Both Stephen and his team of volunteers worked on its restoration and are involved in its operation and maintenance.

The carriages are, in the main, based on the Embsay & Bolton Abbey Steam Railway in Yorkshire, where on many occasions visitors can ride in the Edwardian and/or Victorian vehicles. The six-wheel coaches often run together on selected 'Vintage' and 'Strawberry Specials' days during the summer, and the larger 'saloons' are often attached to the service trains or form part of the railway's hugely popular 'Dales' Dining and Afternoon Tea trains. The Autocar runs in addition to the steam service on selected days and on certain mid-week services.

All exhibits in the collection are more than 100 years old and have fascinating histories. Their incredible stories from construction through working life to withdrawal from service and their subsequent rescue and restoration are the subject of this book.

Stephen Middleton Collection

Stephen Middleton Collection, The Yorkshire Post

The first restoration: GER No 14 - 'A very special Saloon'

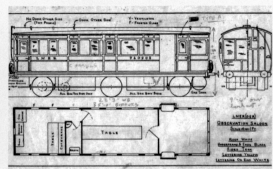

A layout and elevations plan of the coach drawn by Stephen's father as his first project upon joining the LNER District Engineer's department in 1942.

GER No 14 is seen in BR service at Barking on 14 September 1957. It would later be employed as a 'messing van' for workers on the Sheffield electrification project.
Stephen Middleton Collection, H. C. Casserley

Great Eastern Railway saloon No 14 was built at Stratford Works in December 1889 for use by the District Engineer, John Wilson, for inspection purposes. As built it had a varnished teak finish and was the first GER carriage to have electric lighting from new. The observation end had large windows and guard's-type lookouts. The main saloon had fixed couches on either side and a table at the end with a flap to access the lavatory.

In 1897 the body was extended by 4ft 6in to give an attendant's compartment with handbrake, stove and sink, and was mounted on a six-wheel underframe. While at Stratford being used by the District Engineer it is likely that it covered the entire GER system during the course of a year.

Around 1910, in common with royal and other saloons, steam heating was fitted. 1922 saw the centre doors and corridor door sealed and a four-panel Crittall steel window fitted to replace the original three-light arrangement, which included a centre droplight. (This conversion was reversed in preservation, 71 years later, when the carriage was returned to its original appearance.)

In 1925 the saloon was transferred to Ipswich for the District Engineer's use. It was renumbered 960903 in 1947 and stationed at Norwich. Inspection duties ceased when Norwich acquired an ex-GNR invalid saloon that had been converted at Stratford for its new life. This too survives.

No 14/960903 became mobile office accommodation for the electrification of the Great Eastern and London, Tilbury & Southend lines. These were completed in 1960, after which the carriage was transferred to the Sheffield area, where it was used in connection with Woodhead Tunnel inspection duties. In 1973 it was sent to Doncaster for disposal. Little of the interior remained and British Railways had replaced the electric lights with Calor gas. Thanks to the incredible teamwork of John Watling of the GER Society and Sir William McAlpine, this was one of several pre-Grouping saloons saved from scrapping. Following the initial purchase, No 14 spent time at Market Overton and Carnforth before being sold

No 14 at Market Overton on 21 August 1974. Note the four-pane Crittall steel window fitted in 1922.
Stephen Middleton Collection, J. Watling

again to the Rutland Railway Museum, which was later to auction it off (see the Introduction). No restoration was done during this period.

Once Stephen's auction bid had been accepted he had just four weeks to find a site to store the carriage. A retired farmer near Harrogate agreed to house it in a cow shed for £400 a year, and on a cold February Saturday a low-loader eased itself into the shed and the coach was hauled off by a tractor.

Many of Stephen's friends and relatives witnessed the event and questioned his sanity on taking on this 'wreck'. Even he was nervous, having previously not tackled anything larger than O gauge. However, it was now safely under cover and, undeterred, he set a target of Christmas to complete the external bodywork. A joiner replaced areas of rot on bottom frame body timbers, and with a friend Stephen made a new observation end, carefully following the GER drawings provided by John Watling. A few rotten planks on the roof were replaced and a canvas bedded

down onto Williamsons of Ripon special compound. The doors sealed in 1922 were made to open again, and locks, hinges and handles that had been acquired from carriage bodies in March, Cambridgeshire, were fitted. All old panelling was removed and saved to be cut up for beading. (This is one example of Stephen's pragmatic approach to restoration; one railway enthusiast visitor was most critical of this action, suggesting that no matter how split and rotten the panelling was, it should be restored and put back on in the same place, or at least offered to a carriage restorer that would use it as panelling!) Any remaining beads were repaired and templates were made to allow the cutting and shaping of the old panels to make new beads. Toughened glass was bedded on to butyl glazing strip and new beads made for a neat, waterproof job.

The roof had dipped with the weight of the torpedo vents and the removal of the internal partitions years ago. Two half-inch rods with threaded

ends inserted high at partition level squeezed the sides parallel again and straightened the roof. Panels and beads hid the nuts and the rods were concealed by partitions and door frame tops. A few pieces of the original black walnut panelling remained, and from these Stephen reproduced the remainder and fitted them between and above the windows. Below the windows he used Lincrusta, not the original pattern but an appropriate style that is still available. The attendant's compartment was lined out in pine tongue-and-groove wood and painted yellow.

During restoration it was interesting to note that the extension forming the attendant's compartment was not built to as high a quality as the original and was panelled in mahogany. The coach was painted in GER crimson, and Len Clarke gold-lined it as the short lived 1919-22 livery. The underframe was shot-blasted and painted, and the coach cosmetically finished inside and out well in time for its first public appearance.

Stephen Middleton

Stephen Middleton

GER No 14:
a selection of
restoration
progress
photographs. *All
Stephen Middleton*

GER No 14: progress with the internal refurbishment. *All Stephen Middleton*

Above: No 14's first public appearance was at the Eastern Union Railway 150 exhibition at Ipswich in 1996, an event that reinforced the family ties to this area. Stephen's grandfather had been at the centenary exhibition and Stephen still retains the programme for the event that his grandfather took during his spell at Ipswich.

At first many of the carriages on display could only be viewed from the ground with no admittance to the interior. However, setting a trend that Stephen continues to this day, being keen to rightly show off his work, stepladders were found and visitors encouraged to inspect the interiors, where his father took on the role of 'guide', explaining the history of No 14 and his personal memories of the carriage. After welcoming around 2,000 people on board and seeing their reaction, it was clear that No 14 could not possibly be retained in Harrogate for private use – it now had to go to a railway and be enjoyed by a wider public.

John Jolly at Mangapps Farm was kind enough to look after it in the short term.
Stephen Middleton Collection

Above right: GER No 14 was in illustrious steam company at the exhibition. The locomotive line-up (from right to left) was LNER Class 'B12' No 8572, built in 1928 and now resident at the North Norfolk Railway; GER 'T26' Class (LNER 'E4') No 490, built in 1894 and now part of the UK National Collection, on loan to Bressingham Railway Museum; and LNER Class 'N7' No 7999, which was built in 1924 and resides at The East Anglian Railway Museum *Stephen Middleton Collection*

Above: The Mangapps Railway Museum is today a heritage railway centre located near Burnham-on-Crouch in Essex. The three-quarters of a mile of standard-gauge running line and museum are owned and operated by the Jolly family, assisted by volunteers. In June 1997 Stephen was photographed standing proudly next to his carriage. *Stephen Middleton Collection*

Finding a new home: Although there were several expressions of interest, Stephen chose his local line, the Embsay & Bolton Abbey Steam Railway near Skipton. Contractors fitted vacuum brakes and a hand brake to GER No 14, and it arrived on the E&BASR just in time for the Bolton Abbey opening special on 1 May 1998, when it carried previous owner Sir William McAlpine from Embsay to the new station at Bolton Abbey. There Sir William declared the extension open, and the E&BASR expressed its 'appreciation to him and other donors for their generosity'. *All Stephen Middleton*

Strawberry Specials: Following negotiations with the Embsay & Bolton Abbey Steam Railway, No 14 ran a trial of ten summer Saturday evening trains on the understanding that Stephen covered any losses and split profits with the railway 50/50. No 14 has only 16 seats and all were booked in advance; the tickets included strawberries and cream with wine or soft drinks. July 1998 saw the first of these evening trains, illustrated here. Motive power was provided by LNER 'J27' No 65894, which was on loan to the E&BASR from the North Yorkshire Moors Railway. Only able to offer the 16 seats, it barely broke even, but the potential demonstrated that the demand for such a service was there. For financial viability additional capacity was required, therefore a second carriage was needed. *Both Stephen Middleton*

No 14's summer gala outings, 1998

Right: No 14 returns to Embsay from Bow Bridge loop in the hands of 1952-built Andrew Barclay 0-4-0ST No 22. *Author*

Below left: Coupled to an interesting locomotive at Embsay station. *Ann*, which had just returned to service, is a vertical-boilered Sentinel locomotive built in 1927, and believed to be the oldest original example of a Sentinel locomotive. All her working life was spent at British Tar Products at Irlam, near Manchester, until withdrawal circa 1969. *Ann* is now back in Greater Manchester having been sold to volunteers on the East Lancashire Railway, and is undergoing overhaul. *Author*

Below right: No 14 stands in the run-round loop at Bow Bridge with one of the first steam locomotives to arrive on the railway, former NCB 0-6-0ST No S121 *Primrose*. *Stephen Middleton Collection*

Great Eastern Railway No 37

GER Saloon No 37 stands at Blackwell Goods Siding on 20 June 1964. Note that at this stage of its career the centre wheels had been removed.
Stephen Middleton Collection, J. Watling

GER No 37 dates from 1897 and was originally built as a 3rd Class family saloon; it is probably the only survivor of a once numerous type. It was in about as bad a condition as it could be and experts reckoned that it would never run again. However, it made the perfect partner for GER No 14 and could carry 38 passengers. Evidence found during restoration leads to the belief that it was, at some

time, converted for the use of Queen Victoria's granddaughter, Princess Alice. It became clear that luggage racks had been removed to facilitate the fitting of fine American black walnut and all the ceiling beads were plastered in place, silver-leafed and gilded in gold along their edges. This was not a common way to treat a 3rd Class interior!

The carriage was withdrawn from service in July

1939, taking on a role as a barrage balloon men's mess hut in the sidings of London Docks' Pepper Wharf at RAF Blackwall. The centre wheels were removed here because of the gradients and tight curves of the track. It was preserved in 1967 by Saffron Walden MRC and later moved to the East Anglian Railway Museum, where it was placed in storage. Stephen acquired the carriage and rebuilt it from 1998 to 1999.

Below : Around £15,000 was spent within 12 months for a sound but speedy restoration outdoors in the corner of a Harrogate stable's car park. Most of the money went on hiring specialist contractors to replace 70% of the rotten frame. Certainly, this carriage would have been considered beyond *economic* 'traditional restoration', but Stephen's realistic approach means that it is now in a condition that will guarantee many years of use. It can earn its living and maintenance while giving thousands of passengers an enjoyable, educational and unique travel experience. The photographs below and opposite were taken during the restoration process. *Stephen Middleton/Author*

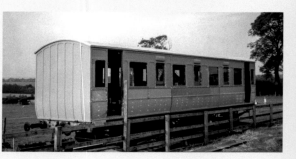

On completion of its restoration, No 37 was transported to the Embsay & Bolton Abbey Steam Railway and paired with No 14. *Cranford No 2* provided the motive power for the first test run for the pair on 12 July 1999. *Stephen Middleton*

Right: No 37 made a lovely partner for No 14 and gave Stephen the additional seating required for the ever-increasing number of 'Strawberry Special' services. On 16 July 2000 1908-built Peckett 0-4-0ST *Annie* was in charge, completing a truly vintage train, seen here arriving at Embsay. *Author*

The artistic skill of painter/signwriter John Furness in evident in December 2019, when No 37 had been further refurbished and was in the process of being fully lined out. Hand painting the lines and lettering was in progress and the fabulous crests were offered up to establish the correct positioning. *Author/Qiuying Middleton*

Great Eastern Railway No 63

GER No 63 was built in 1911 for use by the railway's directors. After 1927 it was employed as an Inspection Saloon in the North East of England and lasted in railway service until 1971. Although passing into heritage railway service and use, for some reason this lovely coach was stripped of its roof covering and side cladding and left for more than ten years exposed to the elements under trees. Sadly this is the fate of so many carriages – good intentions strip out the carriage, then fear takes over as the work and expense involved in restoration bring the project to a halt.

Right: This superb photograph is of GER Directors Saloon No 63 at York during the summer of 1932, while on an engineers inspection train. The locomotive is LNER Class 'X3' (NER '190') 2-2-4T No 190, which itself originally dates from 1849 but was substantially rebuilt in both 1881 and 1894. It was withdrawn in 1936.
Stephen Middleton Collection

Above and top right: GER No 63 was in a rotten condition and at risk when Stephen was offered it for £1. *All Stephen Middleton*

Below and bottom right: No 63 arrives at Harrogate in August 1999. *Stephen Middleton*

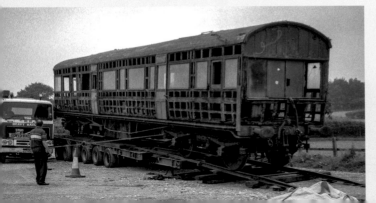

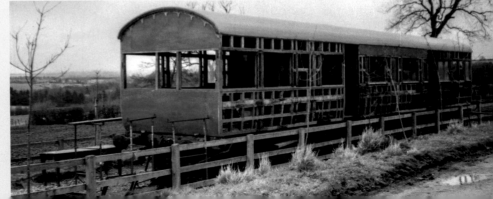

Stephen admits that he only took No 63 because he feared for its future, and as such was not treated as a priority. However, work started in 2000 and as seen in these progress photographs a lot of the main frame timbers had rotted and needed to be replaced. Nevertheless a full restoration was carried out and was just about finished in time for the carriage, looking resplendent, to go to the National Railway Museum's 'outpost' at 'Locomotion', Shildon, County Durham, for a spell, giving passenger rides and taking part in the museum's September 2009 Steam Gala. *All Stephen Middleton*

Left: The impressive and comfortable interior being enjoyed by Stephen and his daughter Honey. *Qiuying Middleton*

A highlight of the Gala event was the pairing of NER No 63 with the iconic LNER Class 'V2' *Green Arrow*, a product of Doncaster Works in 1936. *Stephen Middleton*

Great North of Scotland Railway No 34

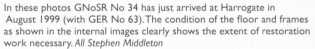

The six-wheeled GNoSR coach No 34 was built in Scotland in 1894 as a 1st Class saloon, but was converted to a Lavatory 1st/3rd Composite carriage in 1909. Its layout was very unusual as, while it was only 36 feet long, it had a corridor, a centre gangway and lavatories. Fine gilding on panels has been reproduced in 1st Class, and Stephen discovered the joys of wood-grain painting as original in the 3rd Class compartments. This coach is so different from English equivalents, and is the only Scottish coach operational in England, and only one of two complete GNoSR carriages left.

Stately Trains bought No 34 in 1999 and transferred it to Harrogate for restoration, which took just over 18 months. It then moved to Embsay, since when it has worked with the two GER six-wheelers. Its internal layout has proved very popular with passengers, and in 2000 it was presented with the Transport Trust's Peter Allen award for restoration.

In these photos GNoSR No 34 has just arrived at Harrogate in August 1999 (with GER No 63). The condition of the floor and frames as shown in the internal images clearly shows the extent of restoration work necessary. *All Stephen Middleton*

In June 2001 the restored coach was transported to Embsay to take its place alongside the two six-wheeled GER carriages Nos 14 and 34. *All Stephen Middleton*

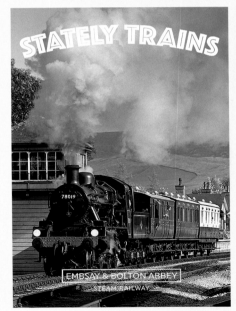

STATELY TRAINS

78019

EMBSAY & BOLTON ABBEY
STEAM RAILWAY

Above: On a very warm 21 August 2013 the now three-coach vintage train looks at home in the Dales landscape behind 0-6-0T *Beatrice*, which was built in Leeds by the Hunslet Engineering Company in 1945. *Author*

Right: An almost timeless scene at Holywell Halt. *Author*

Left: In this image from July 2009 the trio of Stately Trains carriages was behind BR Standard 2-6-0 No 78019, a visitor to the Embsay line from the Great Central Railway at Loughborough. *Author*

On 26 June 2006 the set was in the hands of a preserved diesel with its own interesting history. When built in 1952 by Vulcan/Drewry, the intended use of this ex-BR Class 04 locomotive was as a shunter for BR on the Wisbech & Upwell Tramway, which duty it fulfilled. It is now the last surviving loco to have worked on the tramway. It was Drewry No 2400, and Vulcan Foundry No 145, as well as being BR No 11103, and later D2203, which is the identity it currently carries. While it is now devoid of the sideplates and cowcatchers it would have had in East Anglia, the fixing holes for them are still visible. This loco was almost certainly the basis for 'Mavis' in the hugely popular 'Thomas the Tank Engine' books. *Author*

L&YR No 1 was built in 1906, at Newton Heath, for the directors of Lancashire & Yorkshire Railway, and it is a truly luxurious carriage. Rare Domingan mahogany was used inside, and the red rose of Lancashire and white rose of Yorkshire were incorporated in the tiled mosaic on the lavatory floor.

A photo of Haddon Hall, which was the 1914 prize-winner in the L&Y Horwich apprentices photographic society competition, was displayed in the directors' saloon until 1921. In 1922 the carriage was downgraded to an Inspection Saloon.

Above: This ex-works photo clearly shows the extent of glazing, giving all-round visibility for this Inspection Saloon. Note the folding steps that allowed disembarkation between stations. *Stephen Middleton Collection*

Below: The carriage is offloaded at Draughton on the E&BASR. *All Stephen Middleton*

The coach entered preservation when the North Norfolk Railway bought it and used it as a diesel parts store. The NNR then offered it free to a good home, and in 1999 it was donated to Stately Trains and transferred to the Embsay & Bolton Abbey Steam Railway for restoration. All the original interior mahogany remained in good condition and the underframe was overhauled by a contractor. The interior has retained the mosaic lavatory floor showing the Lancashire and Yorkshire roses entwined. Other original features include carved rare Domingan mahogany porticoes and pillars, etched glass, and even the original long table and apprentices photographic club winning picture of 1914 framed in the smaller saloon (the picture was retained thanks to the Lancashire & Yorkshire Railway Preservation Society).

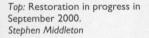

Top: Restoration in progress in September 2000.
Stephen Middleton

Left: Stephen admiring the 1914 photo of Haddon Hall in May 2003.
Stephen Middleton Collection

Above and right:: Stephen and his wife Qiuying apply the finishing touches in May 2003.
Stephen & Qiuying Middleton

Top: Fully restored, the coach stands in the platform at Embsay in October 2008. *Author*

Above: The luxuriously restored interior. *Author*

Right: On 9 August 2001 the newly restored carriage was paired with another Lancashire & Yorkshire veteran. Designed by J.A. F. Aspinall and built at Horwich in 1901, 0-4-0ST No 51218 (L&Y No 68) was specifically designed for shunting tightly curved sidings on the L&YR's dock lines and in goods yards. It is owned by the Lancashire & Yorkshire Railway Trust and based on the Keighley & Worth Valley Railway. It has visited Embsay on a number of occasions. *Stephen Middleton*

Below: Another former Lancashire & Yorkshire Railway locomotive to visit the E&BASR is 'A' Class/Class '27' No 1300 (LMS No 12322, BR No 52322). The opportunity to pair an L&Y coach and locomotive was not to be missed, and this image of the vintage train pulling away from Holywell Halt was taken on 5 May 2014. *Author*

The restored coach has worked several seasons added to E&BASR service trains. For a single journey premium of just £1 it gives public access to what was once an inner sanctum to a privileged few. The coach has also visited the National Railway Museum at York, where it has been a popular exhibit, and featured in the stage production of *The Railway Children* as the Old Gentleman's coach.

Right: On 5 November 2017, with 0-6-0ST *Norman* in service, L&Y No 1 was added to the service train for that optional taste of luxury. *Author*

Left: In 2008 LNER Class 'D49/1' No 246 *Morayshire* visited Yorkshire from its Scottish home at the Bo'ness & Kinneil Railway. It looked the part of the head of vintage train services, with Stately Trains carriages including L&Y No 1 in tow. *Author*

LNWR No 5318 is the youngest and longest of the Stately Trains' carriage fleet. It was built in 1913 for the directors of the London & North Western Railway and as such was lavishly finished. One of the directors was J. Bruce Ismay, also chairman of the White Star Line and survivor of the Titanic sinking. In 1913 it formed part of King George V's Royal Train when visiting Crewe. The coach was divided into saloon compartments on either side of a central block consisting of a toilet, brake compartment and kitchen. Each of the saloon compartments was able to be subdivided into two smaller areas by folding partitions. The largest of the four compartments had a long folding table and a green leather settee nearly 19 feet long. The coach passed into LMS ownership following the 1923 Grouping and was used for inspections by the company's senior management as well as directors. It ran on the trains used to test the LMS pioneer diesels Nos 10000 and 10001 at the end of 1947. The coach suffered slight damage at St Pancras in 1964 and withdrawal followed.

An ex-works image of Saloon No 5318. *Stephen Middleton Collection*

This photograph, from Transport Treasury, is titled 'condemned inspectors saloon coaches'. Stephen acquired a copy of the image for his collection as both coaches are now in his care. No 5318 is in the foreground, with L&Y No 1 behind. The location is a siding opposite Wymondham station in Norfolk and the photo dates from just after both carriages had been withdrawn.
Stephen Middleton Collection, Dr Ian C. Allen, Transport Treasury

Above: Saved for preservation, the coach moved to the North Norfolk Railway, and this photograph shows the carriage being stripped down there. *Stephen Middleton Collection*

Below: The first undercoats are applied to the restored sides. *Stephen Middleton*

Top right and below centre: When the saloon's ownership was transferred to Stately Trains it moved to Embsay in June 2003. Restoration began the following year and was carried out under cover of the carriage shed. Restoration is very much a family affair, as shown here with Stephen's wife well wrapped up as she works on No 5318, while daughter Honey also 'mucked in' under Dad's supervision. *All Stephen Middleton*

Above: One of the coach's six-wheeled bogies under restoration. *Stephen Middleton Collection, Wendy Anderson*

Above: The restored saloon stands at Bolton Abbey station awaiting passengers for a festive afternoon tea on 10 December 2019. *Author*

Left: A rare moment for Stephen as he enjoys the hospitality available.
Qiuying Middleton

Right: Honey Middleton takes a well-deserved break from painting duties to enjoy an afternoon tea.
Qiuying Middleton

Top and above: The spacious interior once utilised by the directors of the London & North Western Railway now provides a lovely environment for afternoon teas. *Author*

The saloon has end windows that, together with the side windows, give passengers magnificent views of the Dales countryside, as seen here on 21 May 2011, when 0-6-0ST Austerity *Norman* was hauling the service train. *Both Author*

East Coast Joint Stock Dining Car No 189

Research reveals that ECJS dining car No189 worked on the London to Aberdeen run, possibly forming part of the trains that were in the informal 'Races to the North', and part of the 'Flying Scotsman' train. It dates from 1894, when British railway companies were introducing dining carriages on their services; before then trains stopped at designated stations where passengers would disembark for meals in the station buffet. They would then return to the train to continue their journey.

Despite being one of the world's oldest surviving dining cars, in January 1998 it was one week away from destruction. No189 had been withdrawn from service in 1927 and sold to a farmer, who used it to house his pigs! It was later acquired by an enthusiast, but he had been fighting a losing battle against the elements. In the winter of 1998 the Vintage Carriages Trust drew Stephen's attention to this Victorian dining car, which was in need of a new home as the landowner wanted rid of it and was about to burn it!

As found, the coach was covered in green mould, had been hit numerous times by forklifts, had been chewed by rats and the roof was letting water pour in. However, most the original detail was there, so Stephen concluded that it was definitely worth saving and bought it in 1998, together with an underframe from a Gresley suburban carriage that was of suitable length.

Above: Just days away from the bonfire, Stephen's first view of the carriage. *Both Stephen Middleton*

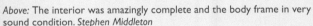

Above: The interior was amazingly complete and the body frame in very sound condition. *Stephen Middleton*

Above centre and above right: The underframe had already been partially scrapped and, together with the carriage, needed to be moved as soon as possible. The Embsay & Bolton Abbey Steam Railway kindly allowed Stephen to bring it to Embsay.

The underframe was the first to arrive, and after much work in finding and fitting suitable missing parts it was set on to Gresley bogies. Two cranes were employed to lift the body from a flatbed lorry onto the underframe – the coach was back on wheels for the first time in 71 years! *Both Stephen Middleton*

Right: Restoration in progress in August 1999. *Stephen Middleton*

Left and far left: A dining car interior depicted on an old postcard, and an artist's impression of Victorian passengers enjoying the 'silver service' of the day. *Stephen Middleton Collection/ Dave Cullingworth*

Below left and below: Exterior restoration was completed by 2003. However, with limited use for the vehicle it was sold and is now owned by the LNER Carriage Association based on the North Yorkshire Moors Railway.

Before heading for the North Yorkshire Moors there was time for an appearance at the 150th Anniversary celebrations at Doncaster Works held over the weekend of 26/27 July 2003.

The photographs were taken during the shunting of the coach in readiness for its journey to Doncaster on a low-loader. *Both Stephen Middleton*

The celebrations in July 2003 marked the 150th anniversary of the Great Northern Railway works at Doncaster. People flocked to the site to view the large number of engines old and new on display, with East Coast Main Line motive power ranging from GNR No 1 and 'A4' 'Pacifics' via 'Deltics' to the then new Class 91.

Above and left: At the Open Day No 189 was coupled as second carriage behind a Victorian locomotive it could well have been hauled by more than 120 years earlier. Stirling 'Single' No 1 was built at Doncaster in 1870 and designed for high-speed expresses between York and London, which could consist of up to 26 passenger carriages. Withdrawn from service in 1907, it was the only example of the class preserved and is part of the National Collection. *Stephen Middleton*

Bottom left: LNER steam royalty, with the world-famous 'A3' *Flying Scotsman*, 'A4' *Union of South Africa* and the Stirling 'Single' in the line-up. *Stephen Middleton*

London & South Western Railway Saloon No 17

LSWR No 17 is the most prestigious carriage in the fleet. Built for the London & South Western Railway's Royal Train in 1885, it was altered to become Queen Victoria's personal coach in her Golden Jubilee year, 1887. She used it when travelling on the LSWR and for her regular trips from Waterloo to Gosport, where she boarded the Royal Yacht that would take her to the Isle of Wight for a stay at her residence on the island, Osborne House. The carriage had two principal saloons separated by a corridor and toilet facilities. At each end of the carriage was a small compartment, one acting as the Queen's boudoir, the other for her attendants.

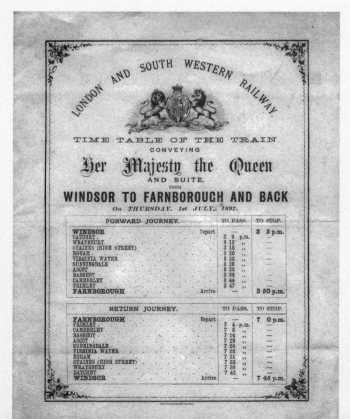

LONDON AND SOUTH WESTERN RAILWAY.

TIME TABLE OF THE TRAIN
CONVEYING

Her Majesty the Queen
AND SUITE,
FROM

WINDSOR TO FARNBOROUGH AND BACK
On THURSDAY, 1st JULY, 1897.

FORWARD JOURNEY.		TO PASS.	TO STOP.
WINDSOR	Depart	—	3 5 p.m.
DATCHET		3 9 p.m.	
WRAYSBURY		3 12 "	
STAINES (HIGH STREET)		3 15 "	
EGHAM		3 20 "	
VIRGINIA WATER		3 23 "	
SUNNINGDALE		3 29 "	
ASCOT		3 33 "	
BAGSHOT		3 38 "	
CAMBERLEY		3 44 "	
FRIMLEY		3 47 "	
FARNBOROUGH	Arrive		3 50 p.m.

RETURN JOURNEY.		TO PASS.	TO STOP.
FARNBOROUGH	Depart	—	7 0 p.m.
FRIMLEY		7 4 p.m.	
CAMBERLEY		7 8 "	
BAGSHOT		7 14 "	
ASCOT		7 19 "	
SUNNINGDALE		7 23 "	
VIRGINIA WATER		7 28 "	
EGHAM		7 31 "	
STAINES (HIGH STREET)		7 35 "	
WRAYSBURY		7 38 "	
DATCHET		7 42 "	
WINDSOR	Arrive		7 45 p.m.

Left: Queen Victoria took a personal interest in the Aldershot Army base from the founding of the camp until the end of her reign. Her husband Prince Albert, the Prince Consort, had been an influential figure in the decision to establish the Army's great training camp at Aldershot, and it was also his initiative to build the Royal Pavilion, just off the Farnborough Road, as a residence for the Queen and members of the Royal Family when they visited the garrison.

The Queen's Diamond Jubilee Review was held at Aldershot on 1 July 1897, and this is the LSWR timetable for the Queen's train journey. 27,000 troops were on parade that day watched by a remarkable assembly of members of the extended Royal Family. Accompanying the Queen were the Prince and Princess of Wales, the Duke and Duchess of York, Princess Victoria of Wales, Prince and Princess Charles of Denmark, the Empress Frederick of Prussia, the Duke and Duchess of Connaught, Prince Henry of Battenberg, the Duchess of Albany, Princess Aribert of Hainault, Princess Victoria of Schleswig-Holstein, and the Duke of Cambridge. Also present were representatives from all over the British Empire and from nearly every state in Europe. Many of these would have travelled with her in this carriage. *Stephen Middleton Collection*

Right: Following Queen Victoria's death in 1901 the carriage continued in royal use for several years before being converted to a family saloon in 1910 and eventually being sold as a body by the Southern Railway in 1930. Kaiser Wilhelm II, the last German emperor, visited in 1907 and travelled on the Royal Train. *Stephen Middleton Collection*

LONDON & SOUTH WESTERN RAILWAY

SPECIAL NOTICE No. 1,821, 1907.

INSTRUCTIONS TO STATION MASTERS, INSPECTORS, ENGINEMEN, GUARDS, SIGNALMEN, PLATELAYERS, GATEMEN, AND ALL OTHERS CONCERNED

AS TO

A SPECIAL TRAIN
CONVEYING

His Imperial Majesty

THE GERMAN EMPEROR
AND SUITE
FROM

HINTON ADMIRAL
TO

WATERLOO,
On MONDAY, 9th December, 1907.

Above: The carriage was withdrawn in 1930 and sent to Selhurst, where it was bought for £70 to form a home, as shown in this photograph. The newly married couple that purchased it lived there for 56 years!

Above right: It was initially bought for preservation in 1989 and, after moving between several preservation sites, it arrived at Embsay in 2006.

Right: At Embsay it was lifted onto a shortened second-hand underframe that had originally been built for a First World War-era London & North Western Railway ambulance train coach. *All Stephen Middleton Collection*

Above and below: These restoration progress photographs include Stephen and Qiuying working on the interior, while daughter Honey and friend paint a clerestory frame. *All Stephen Middleton Collection*

Left and above: Stephen is fortunate to be able to call on the painting and signwriting skills of John Furness, whose free-hand lining, lettering and crests adorn many of the Stately Trains carriages. *Stephen Middleton*

The restoration of this prestigious railway carriage was filmed as part of the Channel 4 Television documentary *Peter Snow's Great Rail Restorations*. The five-part series put the craftsman's art of carriage restoration into sharp focus, and covered the restoration of four classic carriages from different eras. Each coach had its own episode, with the fifth showing all four running together, steam-hauled, in a single unique train on the Llangollen Railway in Wales.

Left: Filming in progress.

Above: Co-presenter Henry Cole with Stephen and Qiuying Middleton.

Above right: Stephen and Qiuying with the main presenter, Peter Snow, in the luxurious surroundings of the completed carriage. *All Stephen and Qiuying Middleton*

Right: The four classic carriages pose alongside the platform at Carrog on the Llangollen Railway. *Stephen Middleton Collection, International Railway Heritage Consultancy Ltd*

Restoration by Stately Trains in 2017 took just six months, as required by the television production team. The carriage is now used on special trains to give passengers a taste of 19th-century royal travel. Passengers can enjoy an assortment of delicacies that were Queen Victoria's favourites while sipping a glass of champagne. This is truly a unique opportunity and passenger numbers are limited to between 18 and 22 depending on the function. The coach is also available for parties, weddings and corporate charter. *Stephen Middleton/Qiuying Middleton/Author*

Above: The Middletons' daughter, Honey, last seen painting carriages on pages 31 and 40, now works 'front of house' serving afternoon teas with her Mum and Dad. *Stephen Middleton Collection, David Oxtaby*

Above: The Stately Trains locomotive, 1916-built 0-6-0ST *Illingworth*, shunts Queen Victoria's Saloon at Embsay. *Stephen Middleton*

QUEEN VICTORIA'S GOLDEN JUBILEE SALOON

EMBSAY & BOLTON ABBEY
STEAM RAILWAY

When restoration is complete, this will be the oldest operational Pullman carriage in the world. It converts from a day car to a sleeper and is the only surviving example of a three-axle Pullman from the four made. This very early car was originally built in America, in kit form, in 1882 for use in France. The order was cancelled, so it came to Britain where the Midland Railway agreed to assemble it. It was then sold on to the Great Northern Railway, but saw very little use. From the GNR it went to the Highland Railway, but was not terribly successful, despite the conventional four-wheel bogies that the Midland Railway had fitted to improve the ride. It was little used after 1906, saw some work during the First World War, and was then withdrawn in 1919. The manager of the Pullman car works at Brighton, himself son of the first Pullman attendant in Britain, was given the carriage body together with that of sister coach *Dunrobin* to make a home upon retirement. He had them lifted off their wheels and mounted them side by side on a proper foundation with a 'traditional' structure between and a timber-framed external wall erected around them. The whole construction was then roofed and clad and the external walls given a rendered finish.

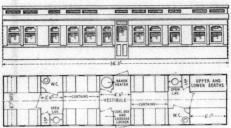

Plan of the Pullman cars "Balmoral" and "Dunrobin," built in 1883 and allocated to the Highland Railway from 1885 to 1907

Above: This elevation and plan of Pullman cars *Balmoral* and *Dunrobin* was drawn in 1957 by C. Hamilton Ellis for a magazine article on the 'Highland Pullmans'. The original is held by the Scottish Railway Preservation Society at Bo'ness. *Stephen Middleton Collection*

The floor plan for the bungalow.

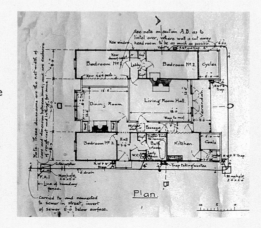

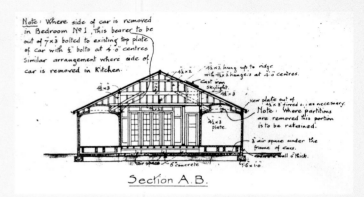

Section A.B.

Above: This section drawing clearly indicates how the carriages were incorporated into the design.

Below: The building under construction in 1920.

Above: The finished bungalow. *All Stephen Middleton Collection, Seaford Museum*

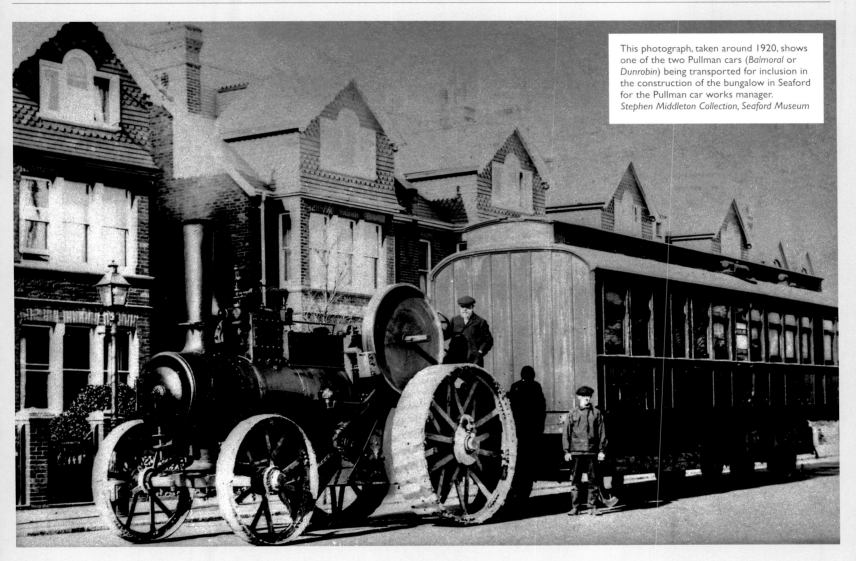

This photograph, taken around 1920, shows one of the two Pullman cars (*Balmoral* or *Dunrobin*) being transported for inclusion in the construction of the bungalow in Seaford for the Pullman car works manager.
Stephen Middleton Collection, Seaford Museum

In the late 1980s, when the bungalow was being demolished, there were initially no takers for the two carriages. By the time a representative from the Brighton Railway Museum took an interest, *Dunrobin* had been 'scrapped', but *Balmoral* was still largely intact, and the museum agreed to take ownership of its body. This was transferred to its base in the former Pullman works at Preston Park. However, financial problems led to the museum's closure.

When Stephen took possession of the coach in 2000 the family of the former owners gave him photos of the demolition works in progress and some interior components retrieved during the works.

As can be seen, the standard of marquetry and glass work is absolutely incredible and the complete interior filled Stephen's garage for a few years. *All Stephen Middleton Collection, Seaford Museum*

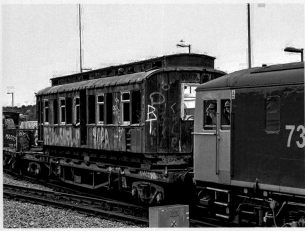

When Stately Trains negotiated title to the body of *Balmoral* it was still residing in the former Pullman car works at Preston Park, Brighton, a building with difficult access. Removal required Network Rail's permission and assistance. With French, American, English and Scottish connections, it is truly a carriage of international significance and, when restoration is complete, will be a superb addition to the fleet.

Top row: At the Pullman car works at Preston Park, Brighton, removal by Network Rail, and arrival at Embsay.

Centre left, left and above: Restoration progress to date. *All Stephen Middleton*

Built as a private saloon in 1877, this was one of the first six-wheel coaches built by the Great Eastern Railway. At that time wealthy families would be able to have their own private railway carriage available for long journeys, and No 8 was classed as a 1st Class saloon, with a compartment for servants as well as luggage space. In 1881 it was converted for the exclusive use of Edward, Prince of Wales. The Great Eastern Railway built a new bogie carriage for the Prince in 1892 and No 8 reverted to a private family saloon. It was withdrawn in the 1920s and became a garden summer house in Essex; it later housed a collection of china, which had to be removed prior to Stephen's purchase.

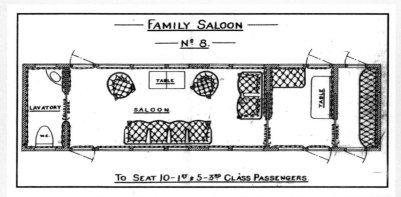

All Stephen Middleton Collection

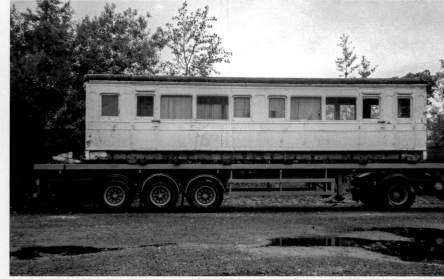

Right: On arrival at the E&BASR the carriage was made watertight, externally 'tidied up' and sited in the Bolton Abbey station car park, as seen in this March 2008 photograph. Here it acted as a fundraiser for the Autocar Trust. *Rob Shaw*

Below and below right: More recently it has been lifted on to a refurbished underframe and transported to Embsay, where it currently resides, protected from the weather awaiting full restoration. *Both Stephen Middleton*

Motive power: NER 1903 petrol-electric Autocar No 3170

At the turn of the 20th century the North Eastern Railway designed and built a pair of 'autocars', which laid the foundation for most of the trains running today. At that time, steam powered the world's railways, and although railcars were being developed, they too were steam powered. These two units were developed to test the theory that if an electrically powered vehicle could carry its own generator with it, there would be no need for additional railway infrastructure such as an electrified third rail or overhead cables. These two experimental railcars, numbered 3170 and 3171 and built between 1902 and 1903, had petrol engines powering generators that worked their electric traction motors, meaning that the vehicles could travel anywhere on the network. This was the world's first use of an internal combustion engine generating electricity for motive power in a passenger-carrying vehicle. The units were also fitted with electric track brakes, another first in railway use. In short, it is hard to overstate the importance of these pioneering vehicles in transport history, as they were 50 years ahead of their time. Similar rail transport did not really take off until the 1950s.

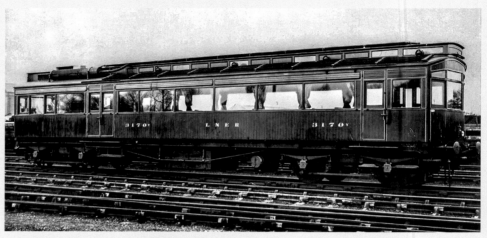

Left: A publicity photo of No 3170. *Stephen Middleton Collection, Ken Hoole Study Centre*

Below left: The NER Autocar attracts interest at Scarborough in the early 1900s. *Stephen Middleton Collection, Ken Hoole Study Centre*

Below: No 3170 leaves Scarborough in around 1904. *Stephen Middleton Collection, Ken Hoole Study Centre*

The Locomotive Magazine, July 11, 1903.]

[Registered at the General Post Office at ...]

273 E.A. Newsum

The LOCOMOTIVE MAGAZINE

And RAILWAY CARRIAGE AND WAGON REVIEW.

Price Twopence Weekly.

Subscription - - - 10s. 6d. per annum post free.
To Foreign Countries - 13s. per annum post free.

Vol. IX.—No. 112.   (Copyright. Entered at Stationers' Hall.)   July 11, 1903.

July 11, 1903.   *The Locomotive Magazine.*   21

No. of tubes in barrel (outside) .. .. 1¾-in. dia.
Heating surface—Tubes .. .. 987 sq. ft.
                 Firebox .. .. 100 ,,
                                    _____
                 Total .. .. 1087 sq. ft.
Grate area .. .. 16.25 ,,

The distributed weights of these engines when rebuilt with new boilers were as given below:—

	Tons.	Cwts.
On bogie	14	4
,, driving wheels	14	12
,, trailing	10	0

No. 30 was broken up in 1896. These engines were known in Mr. Kirtley's official list as class "K," and they are illustrated as rebuilt by him in Fig. 37.

(To be continued.)

MOTOR CARRIAGE, NORTH EASTERN RY.

A CORRESPONDENT has forwarded us a drawing which is here reproduced, showing the general arrangement of the new self-propelled cars with which the North Eastern Railway Company are making experiments on certain branches of their system with a view to substituting this form of vehicle for the ordinary steam locomotive and train. The chief details of construction are shown clearly by reference to the illustration, from which it will be seen that the generating machinery is placed at one end,

seating accommodation is provided for fifty-two passengers in a central compartment, and there is a further division at the rear-end for a conductor or attendant. The motive power is supplied by a petrol motor of the Wolseley type, this having been found to give more satisfactory results than a Napier motor previously tried, which failed to develop its full B.H.P. The engine drives a dynamo direct which generates current for four motors, one on each axle of the vehicle.

The car is of fairly large dimensions, measuring 53-ft. 6-in. in length over the body, or 52-ft. over the headstocks, with a width over the mouldings of 8-ft. 6-in., and an inside breadth of 7-ft. 11¼-in. There is a gangway 2-ft. 1¼-in. wide running the whole length of the passenger compartment, which contains twenty-six lath and space seats with reversible backs, each of which is 2-ft. 10-in. long and 1-ft. 2¼-in. wide, the height above the floor being 1-ft. 5-in. The two bogies have wheels 3-ft. 6-in. in diameter, the wheel centres of each bogie being 8-ft. apart, and the distance between bogie-pin centres 37-ft. 6-in. The end platforms are neatly arranged with rounded fronts, and the sides are plainly finished without any attempt at useless moulding and panelling. The clerestory roof adds to the business-like appearance of the car.

It would be interesting to compare the cost of working a car of this type per passenger unit with that of the steam locomotive and train that it is designed to supersede on local and suburban services.

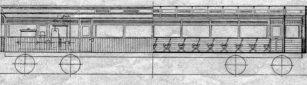

PETROL-ELECTRIC MOTOR CAR, NORTH EASTERN RY.

A fascinating article from *The Locomotive Magazine* of 11 July 1904 describing the 'new self-propelled cars with which the North Eastern Railway Company are making experiments...' *Stephen Middleton Collection*

Below: The Autocar at York in 1904. *Stephen Middleton Collection*

Between 1903 and 1931 No 3170 operated in
Yorkshire and the North East. In 1923, now in
London & North Eastern Railway ownership
following the Grouping, it was fitted with a larger
engine and new generator giving it sufficient power
to pull a conventional carriage, thus increasing
passenger capacity. It was withdrawn from service
in 1931.

No 3170 and a trailer autocoach at Skelton Junction
near York. *Stephen Middleton, Ken Hoole Study Centre*

Luckily, the body of No 3170 was sold to a North Yorkshire landowner and made into a holiday home at Keldholme near Kirkbymoorside on the North Yorkshire Moors. Fitted with a tin roof and veranda it was well protected from the weather and survived there until September 2003, when it was sold to Stephen Middleton, who moved it to the Embsay & Bolton Abbey Steam Railway.

After removal of the tin roof and canopy framework, the original Autocar was revealed. It had been split into two sections and these were lifted onto wagons for transfer to Embsay, where they were placed on a temporary chassis.
All Stephen Middleton

In order to proceed with the complicated restoration of this self-propelled railway vehicle, Stephen and a few volunteers formed a charitable trust, to which ownership of the Autocar was transferred.

After eight years of planning, obtaining parts and recruiting volunteers, the restoration commenced in earnest. Membership increased and, bolstered by grants from the Heritage Lottery Fund, PRISM, the Ken Hoole Trust and a Transport Trust loan, work proceeded rapidly.

THE N.E.R. 1903 ELECTRIC AUTOCAR TRUST

Right: As the original chassis had been scrapped, a similar underframe from a Great Northern Railway milk van was repaired and adapted. The 'new' chassis and power units were assembled at Loughborough on the Great Central Railway, and on 17 March 2016 the first test runs were carried out. *Alan Chandler*

Above and below: Restoration in progress. The interior of the car was in surprisingly in good condition and the original finish was revealed by paint scraping the passenger saloon. *Alan Chandler/Simon Gott*

Left: The chassis was transferred to Embsay in May 2016, and on Friday 22 July the Autocar's body was craned off its temporary underframe and onto the powered chassis. *Alan Chandler*

Work required included the repair/replacement, as necessary, of the timber cladding, and removal of the doors, window frames and droplights for repair/refurbishment. Repairs were required to the roof and a new canvas covering was applied.
Alan Chandler and Colin Clift

On Friday 19 October 2018 the Autocar and its auto-coach were formally launched into service by Sir Ron Cooke, Chair of the Yorkshire & Humber Heritage Lottery Fund Committee, and Stephen Middleton, Chairman of this Trust. Midday saw the Autocar declared operational in front of approximately 150 members and guests, and shuttle services were run from Embsay station to Bow Bridge loop. Later, two return trips were made to Bolton Abbey. The guests and members of the press were very impressed and complimented the quality of the restoration. *All Author*

Right: The railcar's certificate recording its entry in the 'Guinness World Records'.

On 18 April 2019 the Autocar entered public service for the first time and was photographed passing Holywell Halt heading back to Bolton Abbey on the Embsay & Bolton Abbey Steam Railway. *Author*

NER autocoach No 3453

While plans to restore the railcar were in progress, it became clear that its 44-seat capacity could limit its appeal to most heritage railways. It was therefore agreed that an autocoach to run with the Autocar was required.

A partially restored ex-NER autocoach was located on the North Yorkshire Moors Railway. Discussions with its owners, the NER Coach Group, resulted in that group donating the unit to the trust.

The coach had been built at York in November 1904. Originally an eight-compartment 3rd Class coach, it was converted to a 'driving-trailer' Composite Brake coach in December 1906. This allowed it to be coupled to a steam locomotive to form a train that could be driven from the loco or the carriage, hence the autocoach title. This negated the need for the locomotive to run from one end of the train to the other at destination stations.

Below left: An autocoach in service. *Stephen Middleton Collection, K. M. J. Prints of Durham*

Below: This image of an autocoach at Spennymoor station is taken from a postcard produced by the SA Photo Co of Durham and postmarked 25 October 1909. *Stephen Middleton Collection*

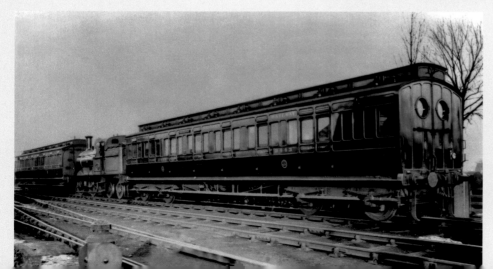

In 2003 Embsay volunteers commenced restoration of the autocoach, which was on its original chassis and had already had some work done at Levisham on the NYMR.

Above left: The autocoach in the sidings at Levisham. *Stephen Middleton Collection*

Above: The autocoach shortly after arrival at Embsay. *Alan Chandler*

Left: The body was repaired and painted, new mouldings applied to the window surrounds, and the roof cleaned and recanvassed. *Alan Chandler*

Above and above right: The completed autocoach. *Alan Chandler*

Right: The autocoach controls. *Author*

The Autocar and autocoach at Bow Bridge loop during one of the shuttle services for invited guests on 'launch' day, 19 October 2018. *Author*

Both air and vacuum brakes have been fitted to the autocoach, enabling it to run with the Autocar or be hauled by a steam locomotive. On 8 September 2019 it formed part of a truly vintage Stately Trains train photographed pulling away from the passing loop at Stoneacre *Author*

Stephen Middleton was surprised to discover that a locomotive from a railway that was local to him and long since closed had managed to survive – the former Nidd Valley Light Railway Hudswell Clarke 0-6-0ST, built in 1916, was in bits in a Norfolk garden.

This diminutive locomotive carried six names during its illustrious career. It was ordered by Bradford Corporation in 1916 but was requisitioned straight from Hudswell Clarke for use at the munitions factory in Gretna Green, where it carried the initials D. E. S. (Department of Explosive Supplies) on the tank. It eventually reached the Nidd Valley Railway in 1923 and was given the name *Mitchell*. When Lewis Mitchell, the company's Chief Engineer resigned, the locomotive was renamed *Illingworth* after his successor. In 1937 it worked at Ebbw Vale steelworks where it was called *Harold*.

Now under the ownership of Sir Robert McAlpine Ltd it carried nameplates bearing the McAlpine name and the number 88. It was sold to Mowlem in 1940 and once again carried out war duties this time at Swynnerton and Ruddington, taking the name *Swynnerton*. In 1946 it worked on the Workington breakwater, then Mowlem's Braehead power station, before being consigned to scrap in 1957. Somehow the engine survived intact, spending half its life as a rusting hulk, passing through several owners but never on public display.

Karl Heath

The locomotive carried the name *Harold* during its stay in South Wales. *Stephen Middleton Collection*

Right: A scrapyard photograph of the rusting *Illingworth*. *Stephen Middleton Collection*

Motive power 2: Hudswell Clarke 0-6-0ST *Illingworth* 63

Below: A fascinating photograph of the locomotive, carrying its original name, *Mitchell*, at Bradford Corporation's Scar House Reservoir works. *Stephen Middleton Collection*

Above: Nearly new Hudswell Clarke No 1208 of 1916 outside St Andrew's Parish Church, Gretna. Note the initials D. E. S. (Department of Equipment and Supplies) on the tank. *Stephen Middleton Collection*

In August 1997 some delicate crane work was required to get the 'kit of parts' loaded up for transportation from Fransham, Norfolk, to Yorkshire. *Stephen Middleton*

Top right and right: Total restoration costs exceeded £200,000, but the loco was virtually complete when Stephen's wife Qiuying ceremonially lit the fire in the boiler for the first time in preservation. Testing on shuttle services was carried out in 2017. *Charles Adams/Stephen Middleton*

Right: On 6 July 2018 the locomotive was officially 'returned to service' at a ceremony that took place at Embsay station. Guest of honour was Tim Illingworth, the great-grandson of local architect and former Lord Mayor of Bradford William Illingworth, after whom the locomotive was named during the construction of Scar House Reservoir. Tim is the current owner of the original nameplates that have been passed down through the generations, having been presented to his great-grandfather when the locomotive was decommissioned. *Stephen Middleton Collection*

Below: Illingworth entered full service in 2019 and can be seen running on the Embsay & Bolton Abbey Steam Railway. On 8 September 2019 it was hauling four carriages from the Stately Trains collection as part of the railway's 1940s Weekend. On this occasion the locomotive was carrying *Sir Robert McAlpine & Sons No 88* nameplates. *Author*

Stately trains on tour

Right: **NORTH NORFOLK RAILWAY** The popularity of the original pair of restored Great Eastern Railway carriages extended well beyond Embsay, and they were hired by the North Norfolk Railway and North Yorkshire Moors Railway (twice), proving very popular with their crews and visitors.

In December 2001 they were photographed at Sheringham station on the North Norfolk Railway on a 'Christmas Platter Special'. Great Western Railway pannier tank No 9682, built in 1949, was the motive power. *Stephen Middleton*

Left: **NORTH YORKSHIRE MOORS RAILWAY** 19th-century splendour on the NYMR, with the Furness Railway Trust's 0-4-0 No 20, dating from 1863, hauling GER carriages Nos 14 and 37. The train is approaching Newbridge on its way from Pickering to Levisham in October 2000. *Author*

Above: **RETURN TO MID-SUFFOLK** On 6 April 1952 GER No 14 was photographed on the Mid-Suffolk Railway between Laxfield Mill and station. The 'J15', No 65467, was built at Stratford Works in 1912 and, following its working life based at Ipswich and Stratford sheds, returned there for disposal in 1959.
Stephen Middleton Collection, Dr Ian Allan

Right: In July 2002 the North Norfolk Railway's newly restored GER Class 'Y14'/LNER Class 'J15' 0-6-0 BR No 65462 visited the Mid-Suffolk Light Railway for its very first steam weekend, and GER No 14 returned to join the celebrations, 50 years after the earlier photograph was taken. The 'J15' was renumbered as sister locomotive No 65447, which had been based at Ipswich shed for its working life. The setting is Brockford & Wetheringsett station. *Stephen Middleton*

NORTH YORKSHIRE MOORS RAILWAY 2 A second visit to the NYMR saw Great Eastern Railway carriages Nos 14 and 37 joined by Great North of Scotland Railway No 34. Here they are seen at Levisham with 0-6-0ST *Cranford. Stephen Middleton*

WENSLEYDALE RAILWAY The restored LNER Directors Saloon has visited the Wensleydale Railway, and is shown here being shunted by Class 47 No 47715 *Haymarket. Stephen Middleton*

Left: **DONCASTER WORKS:** In July 2003 Lancashire & Yorkshire Railway Directors Saloon No 1 was on display at Doncaster Works as part of the celebrations of the 150th Anniversary of the Great Northern Railway works.

Right: **THE WENSLEYDALE RAILWAY:** While at Wensleydale Rishi Sunak, MP for the local Richmond constituency, enjoyed an afternoon tea alongside the Middletons in the Directors Saloon. Did he know then that he would go on to become Chancellor of the Exchequer and have to deal with the financial consequences of a worldwide pandemic? *Stephen Middleton Collection, International Railway Heritage Limited*

Below: **LLANGOLLEN RAILWAY** The culmination of the Channel 4 television series that followed the restoration of four vintage carriages was the running of a special train on the Llangollen Railway in mid-Wales. All four coaches were transported to the railway and were filmed running together along the line behind a steam locomotive. Stately Train's London & South Western Railway 1st Open No 17 (Queen Victoria's carriage) was joined by the 1864-built Isle of Wight Railway No 10, Gresley Brake Composite No 4229 and the 1960-built Metropolitan-Cammell 1st Kitchen Pullman car No 311 *Eagle*.

The four were photographed travelling through the wonderful Welsh landscape behind Great Western 'Large Prairie' No 5199. *Stephen Middleton Collection, International Railway Heritage Consultancy Ltd*

Above: Shunting the vintage stock in Pentrefelyn carriage and wagon sidings. *Stephen Middleton Collection, Stephen Fletcher*

Left: **PONTYPOOL & BLAENAVON RAILWAY** For its Autumn Steam Gala in September 2019, the South Wales railway played host to 0-6-0ST *Illingworth*, which was carrying the name *Harold* to reflect the time it spent working at Ebbw Vale. Stately Trains' Great Eastern Railway carriage No 63 was also at the railway and the opportunity to pair it with *Illingworth* could not be resisted. *Stephen Middleton Collection/, Matt Anderson*

Above: **MID-SUFFOLK LIGHT RAILWAY** In 2018 *Illingworth* visited the Mid-Suffolk line for its gala. *Karl Heath*

Awards

The full list of awards received by Stephen Middleton/ Stately Trains up to the end of December 2019 is as follows:

1996   Association of Independent and Preserved Railways (now HRA) award, GER District Engineers coach, built 1889

1998   Transport Trust Restoration Award for GER family saloon, built 1896

2000   Heritage Railway Association, Outstanding Contribution to Railway Preservation

2000   Transport Trust, Peter Allen Award for GNoSR carriage, built 1894

2004   Yorkshire Forward Enterprise Award, Stately Trains

2006   Transport Trust David Muirhead Award, GER Directors Saloon, built 1911

2007   Museums and Heritage Awards for Excellence, Stately Trains

2009   Transport Trust Restoration award for LNWR Directors Saloon, built 1913

2014   Transport Trust Restoration award for autocoach, built 1904, Autocar Trust

2016   Guinness World Record: 'The first internal combustion electric railcar was built in York in 1903 … only survivor today and operates on tourist and preserved historic railways.'

2017   Transport Trust, David Muirhead Award, LSWR Queen Victoria's Saloon, built 1885

2019   Heritage Railway Association Manisty Award to Autocar Trust: 'The Association's most prestigious award. Awarded by the Board of the HRA on an occasional basis for an exceptional and outstanding contribution to railway preservation. It is not possible to make any nomination for this Award.'

2019   Modern Traction Award, Autocar Trust

2019   Sir William McAlpine Award, Autocar Trust

WARLEY MODEL RAILWAY EXHIBITION: NER petrol-electric Autocar No 3170 was the star attraction at the annual Warley Model Railway Exhibition in 2019, held at the NEC in Birmingham. The Autocar had already received the top honour of the Heritage Railway Association Awards, the Peter Manisty Award for Excellence, for its restoration. While at the show No 3170 was presented with the Association of Larger Scale Modellers Ltd's Sir William McAlpine Award for the best preservation project in 2019, representing the latest in a long line of awards bestowed upon restoration projects instigated by Stephen. *Author*

Film and television

The vintage collection assembled under the Stately Trains banner has attracted the interest of film, television and theatre producers over the years, and carriages have been used in a variety of film, photographic and theatrical productions.

AGATHA Before becoming a part of the collection, the Great Eastern Railway Saloon No 63 was photographed at the rear of a *Flying Scotsman*-hauled train travelling from Carnforth to York for the filming of the 1979 motion picture *Agatha*, which starred Dustin Hoffmann and Vanessa Redgrave. *Stephen Middleton Collection*

Right: **JERICHO** In 2016 the Embsay & Bolton Abbey Steam Railway featured in ITV's period drama *Jericho*. This was a period drama mini-series set in the fictional town of Jericho, a shanty town in the Yorkshire Dales that has sprung up around the construction of a railway viaduct in the 1870s. The series reimagines the story of the building of the Ribblehead Viaduct, which was renamed the Culverdale Viaduct in the show. Great Eastern Railway carriages Nos 14 and 37 were part of the set, which also included the Vintage Carriages Trust's 0-6-0 saddle tank *Sir Berkeley*, which dates from 1890. *Courtesy of the Yorkshire Dales Railway Museum Trust Archive*

Above and right: **POSSESSION** This 2002 Warner Bros film included scenes filmed on the North Yorkshire Moors Railway. GER carriages Nos 14 and 37 were included in the vintage train, which was hauled by the oldest working standard-gauge steam locomotive in Britain, the Furness Railway Trust's No 20, which dates from 1863. *Both Stephen Middleton*

Right: **GREAT BRITISH RAILWAY JOURNEYS** In 2010, for the then new BBC television documentary series, Michael Portillo took to the tracks with a copy of George Bradshaw's Victorian railway guidebook. In a series of epic journeys, Portillo travelled the length and breadth of the country to see how the railways have changed us, and what of Bradshaw's Britain still remained. As part of Series 1, in Episode 3 Michael travelled back in time on the Embsay & Bolton Abbey Steam Railway in one of the Stately Trains vintage carriages, meeting Stephen and his family during the recording of the programme.

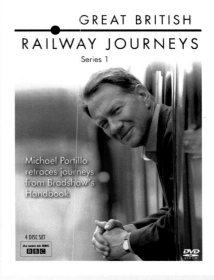

OLIVIER AWARD-WINNING PRODUCTION OF

E. NESBIT'S **THE RAILWAY CHILDREN**

★★★★★
THE GUARDIAN

★★★★★
WHATS ON STAGE

YORK THEATRE ROYAL PRODUCTION
IN ASSOCIATION WITH THE NATIONAL RAILWAY MUSEUM

DVD
VIDEO

U

Right, below right and below: Great North of Scotland Railway No 34 performed in the purpose-made theatre behind King's Cross station in London.
Stephen Middleton

Above: **THE RAILWAY CHILDREN** E. Nesbit's cherished novel was, in 2008, brought to life in an Olivier Award-winning adaptation from the York Theatre Royal. The stage adaptation was initially held at the National Railway Museum in York, but such was its success that it also transferred to King's Cross station in London, where a purpose-built theatre was constructed. The show was later to return to York. Carriages from the Stately Trains collection had starring roles in both productions.

Above centre and above right: London & North Western Railway and Lancashire & Yorkshire Railway Directors Saloon No 5318 starred in the National Railway Museum's production in York. *Stephen Middleton*

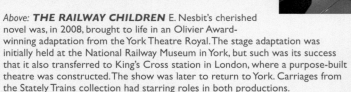

Great Eastern Railway No 63 had the honour of representing Stately Trains in Canada. The production had been shipped across the sea to Toronto where a purpose-built theatre with 1,000 seats was constructed in Roundhouse Park beneath the CN Tower and next to the Rogers Centre, which stands on former railway land. The 'Roundhouse' is a preserved locomotive roundhouse that is home to the Toronto Railway Museum. Between performances former London & South Western Railway 'T3' Class 4-4-0 locomotive No 563 and the GER carriage were posed on the large turntable. *All Stephen Middleton*

Glyndyfrdwy Station House

Glyndyfrdwy is an intermediate station on the Llangollen Railway in Mid-Wales. This heritage railway runs through the beautiful Dee Valley. On closure of the line by British Rail in 1968, the station buildings became a private house. When the Llangollen Railway rebuilt and reopened the line, the station became a crossing point for the heritage steam trains.

In 2011 Stephen Middleton bought the station buildings and refurbished them. On the station's website Stephen explains what makes it so special to the Middleton family:

'The station is well off the main road so it is quiet. It truly is like stepping back 50 years. My daughter loves the butterflies in summer and skimming stones in the nearby River Dee. My wife enjoys the garden, the great pub nearby and the clean air. Me? Well even now I cannot help but stop what I am doing and rush to see the grand old trains.'

The property is available for private hire and visitors will enjoy sharing some of the Middletons' treasured possessions such as the Pullman chair and the tick of the station clock during their break at this wonderful station. Further information search www.stationholiday.co.uk.

All photos Stephen Middleton/Christmas card artwork, M. J. Cousins

The Stately trains collection today

E&BASR 1940S WEEKEND, 2019
On 8 September 2019 *Illingworth*, carrying
the name *Sir Robert McAlpine & Sons No 88*,
hauled three carriages from the Stately Trains
collection together with the Autocar Trust's
NER autocoach – they were Great Eastern
Railway No 14, Great North of Scotland
Railway No 34 and North Eastern Railway
autocoach No 3453, with Queen Victoria's
London & South Western Railway No 17 at
the back. *Author*

Carriages from the Stately Trains collection
provided a period backdrop for the many and
various re-enactors who attended the event.
Author

Left and centre below: E&BASR/STATELY TRAINS 2020: After the initial three-month lockdown in response to the Coronavirus pandemic, the E&BASR made preparations to reopen on 25 July 2020 with all appropriate Covid-19 precautions in place. Steam trains and Dales Dining services were run every Tuesday, Saturday and Sunday from 25 July onwards. Customers were more spread out than usual to provide social distancing between groups, and stringent cleaning procedures were put in place for the benefit or customers and staff. The Stately Trains locomotive Illingworth hauled the 'reopening' services on 25 July.

To mark the courage of all those in the front line tackling the Covid-19 pandemic the railway announced that the 1916-built Illingworth would be renamed Nightingale and Seacole. A naming ceremony would be held in 2021, as soon as it was judged to be safe, and it is hoped that the railway, together with others in the wider community, will take the opportunity to remember this time for current and future generations.

Representatives of the Florence Nightingale Foundation and the Mary Seacole Trust will unveil the nameplates. This is particularly appropriate as the Florence Nightingale Foundation is marking 200 years since Florence Nightingale's birth with the White Rose appeal.

Left and right: '1940s WEEKEND': Having been withdrawn from service in 2019, the superbly refurbished LNWR Directors Saloon No 5318 emerged from the 'works' in 2020 to take its place on the post-lockdown trains. Delicious afternoon teas were served on selected services. On 12 September, during the railway's '1940s Weekend', suitably attired re-enactors were photographed enjoying their refreshments beneath the highly appropriate 'White Star Line' poster that proudly hangs on the wall in the saloon.